A Gap in Nature

Discovering the World's Extinct Animals

Tim Flannery & Peter Schouten

Atlantic Monthly Press

New York

OTHER BOOKS BY THE AUTHORS
Possums of the World: A Monograph of the Phalangeroidea
Tree Kangaroos: A Curious Natural History with R. Martin & A. Szalay

TIM FLANNERY
Mammals of New Guinea
The Future Eaters: An Ecological History of the Australasian Lands and People
Mammals of the South West Pacific and Moluccan Islands
Watkin Tench, 1788 ed.
The Life and Adventures of John Nicol, Mariner ed.
Throwim Way Leg: Tree-Kangaroos, Possums, and Penis Gourds
The Explorers: Stories of Discovery and Adventure from the Australian Frontier
The Birth of Sydney ed.
Terra Australis: Matthew Flinders' Great Adventures in the Circumnavigation of Australia ed.

PETER SCHOUTEN
Prehistoric Animals of Australia, S. Quirk & M. Archer eds.
The Antipodean Ark: Creatures from Prehistoric Australia, S. Hand & M. Archer eds.

First published in Australia in 2001 by The Text Publishing Company

Published simultaneously in Canada
Printed in Singapore

Library of Congress Cataloging-in-Publication Data
    Flannery, Tim F. (Tim Fridtjof), 1956–
    A gap in nature: discovering the world's extinct animals / Tim Flannery; illustrated by Peter Schouten.
        p. cm.
        ISBN 0-87113-797-6
        1. Extinct animals. I. Schouten, Peter. II. Title.

    QL88 .F54 2001
    591.68—dc21   2001033668

Book Design by Chong Wengho
Map drawn by Peter Schouten, based on the map *Typus Orbis Terrarum* by Abraham Ortelius-Antwerp, 1570

Atlantic Monthly Press
841 Broadway
New York, NY 10003

01 02 03 04   10 9 8 7 6 5 4 3 2

To Mark O'Brien
without his patience and support this book would never have materialised

Acknowledgments

We wish to acknowledge the help of the following people, who provided access to collections under their care, checked facts, or supplied information during the course of this work: Steve Donnellan, Mark Hutchinson, Marianne Anthony, Phillippa Horton (South Australian Museum, Adelaide); Walter Boles, Ross Sadlier, Sandy Ingleby, Carol Cantrell (Australian Museum, Sydney); Diana Jones (Western Australian Museum, Perth); Colin Groves (Australian National University, Canberra); Ken Hill, Alan Millar (Royal Botanic Gardens, Sydney); Geoff Tunnicliffe (Canterbury Museum, Christchurch); Alan Tennyson (Dominion Museum [Te Papa], Wellington); Ross MacPhee, Clare Flemming, Alison Andors (American Museum of Natural History, New York); Leo Joseph (The Academy of Natural Sciences, Philadelphia); Rene Dekker, Chris Smeenk (Naturalis Museum, Leiden); Nick Arnold, Paula Jenkins (Natural History Museum, London).

Contents

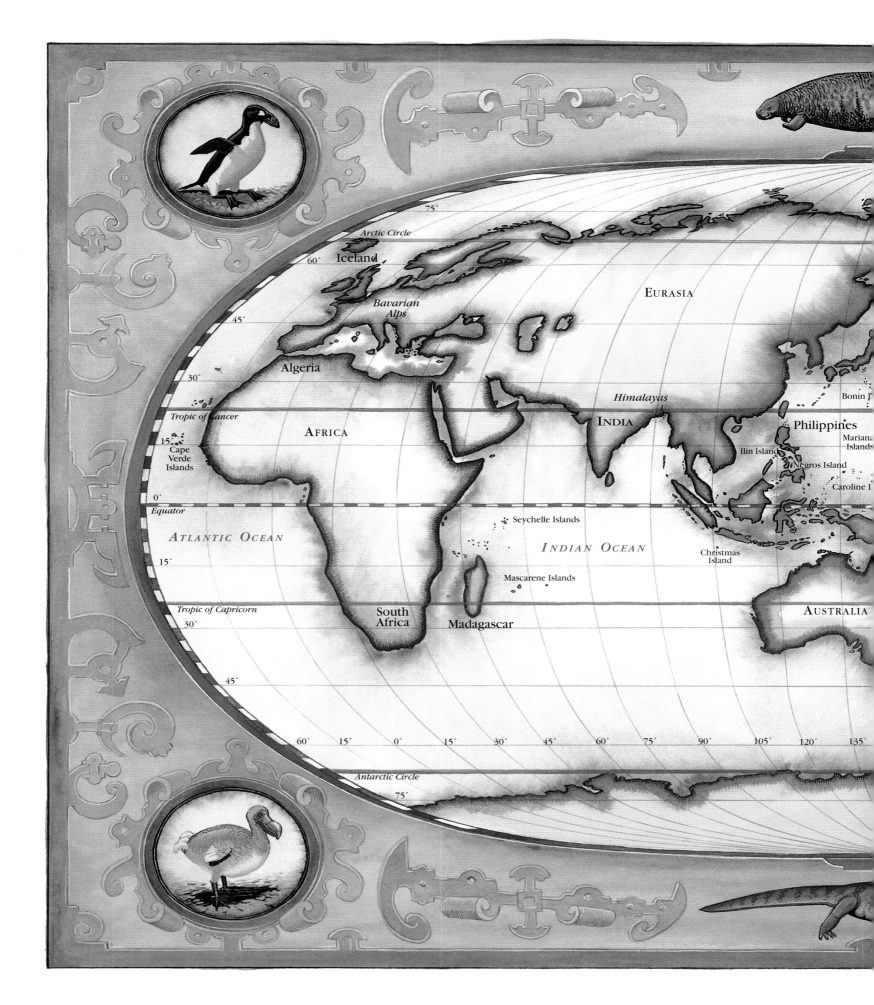

75°

Arctic Circle

60° Iceland

EURASIA

45°

Bavarian Alps

30°

Algeria

Himalayas

Tropic of Cancer

AFRICA

INDIA

Philippines

Bonin I

15°
Cape
Verde
Islands

Mariana
Islands

Ilin Island

Negros Island

0°

Caroline I

Equator

ATLANTIC OCEAN

Seychelle Islands

INDIAN OCEAN

Christmas
Island

15°

Mascarene Islands

Tropic of Capricorn

South
Africa

Madagascar

AUSTRALIA

30°

45°

60°   15°   0°   15°   30°   45°   60°   75°   90°   105°   120°   135°

Antarctic Circle

75°

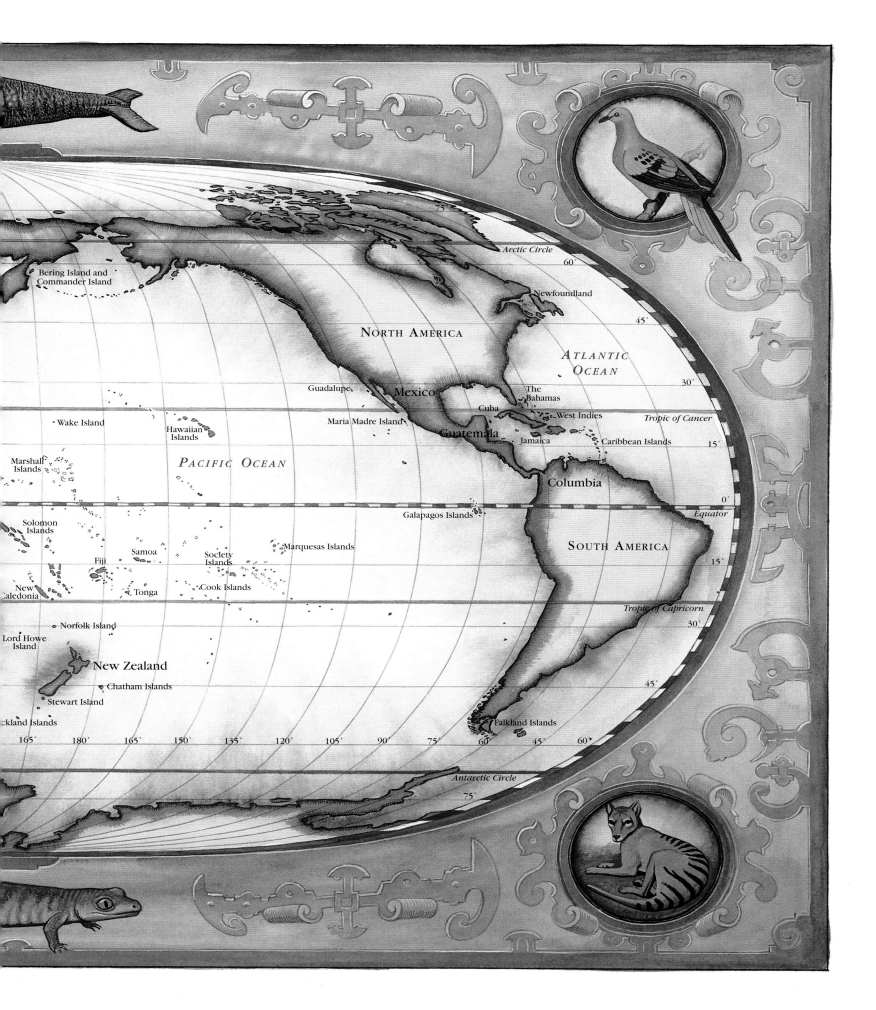

Bering Island and
Commander Island

Newfoundland

NORTH AMERICA

ATLANTIC
OCEAN

Guadalupe

Mexico

The
Bahamas

Cuba

Wake Island

Maria Madre Island

West Indies

Tropic of Cancer

Hawaiian
Islands

Guatemala

Jamaica

Caribbean Islands

Marshall
Islands

PACIFIC OCEAN

Columbia

Solomon
Islands

Galapagos Islands

Equator

SOUTH AMERICA

Marquesas Islands

Samoa

Fiji

Society
Islands

New
Caledonia

Tonga

Cook Islands

Tropic of Capricorn

Norfolk Island

Lord Howe
Island

New Zealand

Chatham Islands

Stewart Island

Falkland Islands

ckland Islands

165°   180°   165°   150°   135°   120°   105°   90°   75°   60°   45°   60°

Arctic Circle   60°
45°
30°
15°
0°
15°
30°
45°

Antarctic Circle
75°

An Age of Extinction

by Tim Flannery

In an account of a 1598 Dutch voyage to the Mascarene Islands is a crude drawing titled 'the destruction of the dodos'. At its foot are printed a few lines of doggerel that were translated into English late in the nineteenth century:

For food the seamen hunt the flesh of feathered fowl,
They tap the palms, the round-sterned dodo they destroy,
The parrot's life they spare that he may scream and howl,
And thus his fellows to imprisonment decoy.

The words of this ancient rhyme seem inexplicable. What, the reader asks, could tapping of palms have to do with hunting dodos, and why would a screaming parrot attract rather than repel its fellows? The words make sense only if one knows a little about virgin isles—places that have escaped the fatal impact of humans. When it was first visited by the Dutch in the early sixteenth century Mauritius, home of the dodo, was one such place. Not only were people unknown there, but it had no mammalian inhabitants at all, except a few bats. Its dodos and parrots had never been hunted, except perhaps by hawks when nestling. They consequently knew no fear of those Dutch sailors, whose hollow tapping on palm trunks may have sounded like the dodo's call (which incidentally was never recorded), or perhaps attracted the great birds by its novelty alone. Whatever the case, it is clear from early accounts that hunting dodos was as simple as getting their attention and carrying them on board ship.

The island's parrots flocked to the cries of a wounded mate, thus enabling hunters to trap them in their thousands. The 'destruction of the dodos' conjures activities that would happen repeatedly over the next four centuries, as humans discovered one innocent isle after another, and obliterated their extraordinary inhabitants.

It was not only the world's islands that would be affected by terrible extinctions over those centuries. Just 160 years ago tens of millions of hooves churned the American plains as vast herds of buffalo thundered across them, while in the continent's eastern forests flocks of hundreds of millions of passenger pigeons streamed by, taking hours to pass. Then, the snows of New York winters were enlivened with flights of parakeets and Tasmanians knew the dog-like thylacine, while dozens of curious bandicoots, wallabies and native rats filled Australia's inland plains. Every continent has suffered extinctions at the hands of the European expansion, leaving them all impoverished in comparison with their recent past.

It may seem a soul-destroying task to set about documenting, in words and pictures, these creatures which have all perished in the last 500 years; but this project is one of the most exciting I have ever been involved in. That's because it has allowed me to glimpse, in my imagination at least, a tiny flicker of the wonder of this lost world. Each time I visited Peter Schouten, my collaborator in this work, a few more long-lost animals had emerged onto his canvas. Often this was a revelation, for I had never before seen an accurate illustration of them. Some indeed were species that no one had seen—except as distorted or fragmentary museum specimens—for decades or even centuries.

Peter's paintings are life-sized in the original, and I often felt as I gazed at them that I was looking at the living creature for the first time. Upon viewing Schouten's dodo I realised that every other illustration of the creature I had seen was a mere caricature. To behold Steller's sea cow—all eight metres of the beast, in intricate detail—makes one aware as nothing else can just how terrible a loss its extinction was. On seeing his huia, I imagined its call, and in my mind heard the myriad dawn chorus that once resounded on hundreds of Pacific islands, the likes of which will be no more. Each illustration Peter completed over the four years of the project was a voyage of discovery—an investigation of a creature accessible in no other way—for there are no photographs of most species illustrated here, and the few that are available are in black and white.

Because it was essential for Peter to create images that would be as accurate as possible, we both made numerous trips to museums that held relevant specimens. There we would photograph, sketch and make notes on the faded and distorted specimens; and these records, along with written accounts and sketches drawn from life, made up the reference materials we needed for the artwork and text. Such research was often wonderfully exciting. On occasion I would find myself descending into the vault of some European museum where the rarest and most valuable specimens are housed. There a curator would unlock a cabinet and open a drawer to reveal a stuffed bird skin that the great Captain James Cook himself had seen—the sole example sometimes of an entire species. On one memorable occasion at Oxford University the famous dodo head was placed reverently in my hands, and on another I peered through an alcohol-filled jar at the sad remnants of a long-extinct fruit-bat. To see or touch such specimens seemed to put me into direct contact with a rich, now vanished world, which could only be resurrected by my collaboration with Peter.

As Peter sat sketching, his mind would fill with a vision of the creature as it must have been in life. We would talk about the habitat of the virgin isle or unexplored desert that had once been its home and gradually a sense of the animal in its environment would emerge. Work on painting and text would begin when both of us felt confident that we understood what this species must really have been like.

Extinction must be regarded over the vastness of evolutionary time as the fate of all species—as unavoidable as death and taxes. Some people, economists among them, have used this insight to argue that there is no need to worry about the extinction of species in the modern world. Theirs, however, is a flawed reasoning, for there are periods in history when the rate of extinction is so rapid that whole ecosystems are destabilised and swept away. Then the earth becomes a less productive, less stable and more impoverished place.

Our present age is one such time, and it is our species that has brought things to their present, sorry state; for this is, as Richard Leakey so ably put it, the sixth age of extinction. The last time the planet experienced a comparable carnage was 65 million years ago during the demise of the dinosaurs, and just four times previously over half a billion years of evolutionary time have extinctions on this scale occurred. This sixth age of extinction did not begin, as you might imagine, with the arrival of the industrial era a few hundred years ago. Instead it first dawned at least 50,000 years earlier, when our species first left its African cradle and began its spread across the face of the Earth, precipitating other living forms into oblivion by the dozen. We cannot be certain, of course, about anything that happened so long ago, but evidence is growing that a common thread runs through the extinctions of the last fifty millennia, and that Homo sapiens, either directly or indirectly, is that thread.

Today at many places in North and South America, Australia, Asia and Europe, you can dig into the earth and find the bones of enormous creatures which existed up until the time that fully modern humans arrived. The astonishing size and abundance of these remains caused Alfred Russel Wallace, the co-founder of the theory of evolution by natural selection, to expostulate that 'we live in a zoologically impoverished world, from which all the hugest, and fiercest, and strangest forms have recently disappeared'.

Wallace had no idea what caused the extinction of all of these huge, fierce and strange creatures, nor indeed when they died out. Today we have a much clearer picture of the catastrophe that impoverished the planet.

Australia, we now know, was the first continent to be stripped of its giants. It lost over sixty species of marsupials, reptiles and flightless birds, including rhino-sized marsupial diprotodons, massive kangaroos, six-metre-long goannas and horned tortoises as long as a Volkswagen Beetle. Many if not all were swept away at around the time the ancestors of the Aborigines arrived on the continent, some 46,000 years ago. Europe's extinctions were more modest, and appear to have occurred later—around 30,000 years ago—by which time the ancestors of the modern Europeans had wrested most of the continent from the Neanderthals. By around 14,000 years ago humans had pushed far into Eurasia's boreal north, invading the tundra and mammoth steppe that covered untold square kilometres of the world's largest continent. These invaders rapidly drove mammoth, woolly rhino and giant elk, among others, into oblivion.

Then, just 13,200 years ago, before the world's sea level rose as the ice age waned, bands of hunters crossed the Bering land bridge into a new world, inheriting at a sweep nearly 30 per cent of the globe's habitable land surface. In North America, a big-game hunting culture known as Clovis rapidly took shape and another continent was emptied of its fiercest, largest and strangest creatures. Sabre-toothed cats known as smilodonts, Columbian mammoths, mastodonts, gigantic sloths, condor-like teratorns and the new-world horse all fell victim in just a few hundred years. South America was likewise devastated, losing its tank-like glyptodonts, its sloths and many other bizarre animals.

Thus, in its first forty millennia, the sixth extinction ran a wild and deadly course, exterminating the world's giants. Australia lost 95 per cent of its land-animal genera weighing more than forty-five kilograms, and the Americas 75 per cent. Losses in Europe and Asia were more modest, at around 30 per cent. Paradoxically, Africa alone—the nursery of our destructive species—was the only continent to escape without significant loss. Just a few species, such as a giant water buffalo, a relative of the black rhino and a warthog became extinct. This paradox may be explained by the fact that Africa was humanity's training ground. It was there that we first learned to kill the large mammals, and that slow process gave Africa's bigger creatures the chance to adjust to the habits of ever more efficient human hunters.

A second phase of extinction began when humans left the continents and began to colonise the world's islands. Some, such as New Guinea, were probably settled at around the same time as their nearest continent (in this case Australia), but this extended form of colonisation began to accelerate around 10,000 years ago, when people started to spread through the islands of the Mediterranean. There, on some of the most beautiful places on earth, they encountered a very strange new fauna— pygmy hippos and waist-high elephants, short-legged deer and enormous eagles. Just imagine how many tourist dollars it would be worth to Cyprus today if the ancient Cypriots had spared just a few of the island's pint-sized elephants; or how much it would mean to Crete if gigantic eagles still soared in Cretan skies.

By around 6000 years ago the Indian inhabitants of the Americas reached the Caribbean. They too encountered weird fauna: huge flightless owls and ground sloths on the large islands like Cuba, and rodents the size of black bears on some smaller ones. It is likely that tens if not hundreds of species vanished from the Caribbean islands at this time. Palaeontologists are still counting the toll.

Just what those vanished island menageries were like can hardly be imagined today, for not a single drawing, not one mummified pelt or stray feather of any of those animals survives. Yet, from what we know of island creatures everywhere, we can speculate on their temperaments and diet. Islands offer a limited array of resources and larger creatures have to be flexible to survive in such places. Thus it is almost certain that most of the bigger species had broad feeding habits. Islands also possess a limited array of predators, so many species are rather slow and unafraid. To judge from the few island giants that survived into the historic period, these creatures would have acted as if they were tame when they met their first humans. They would not have run away, but perhaps curiously approached their destroyers. In a wiser world they might have made perfect pets, or even domestic livestock.

The despoliation of those island archipelagos within easy reach of the continents was, however, merely a beginning; for the numerous islands in the Pacific beckoned to more adventurous sea farers. To them, the scattered oceanic islands were immense larders, stocked over millions of years by creatures which had evolved in isolation after somehow reaching their distant homes. These animals too were exquisitely vulnerable to human disruption. Around three and a half thousand years ago the ancestors of the Polynesians began colonising these miniature worlds. They spread relentlessly through the Pacific, hardly an island escaping their keen navigational skills, until even remote Henderson Atoll in the far east, and the Chatham Islands east of chilly New Zealand, had been sought out and settled.

On every archipelago they encountered a plethora of unique life, and palaeontologists believe that by 500 years ago they had eaten their way through an estimated 2000 species of birds alone. Today just 8000 bird species survive worldwide, so the Polynesian expansion cost the planet one out of every five species that existed at the time it commenced. Among them were giants of almost every description: pigeons the size of turkeys, scrub turkeys as big as sheep, parrots as large as small dogs, and of course New Zealand's renowned moa, some of which grew to nearly three metres high.

Around 1500 years ago the ancestors of the Polynesians made a spectacular journey in a completely unanticipated direction, during which they discovered the most biologically special island on the planet. Instead of heading out across the Pacific they crossed the great expanse of the Indian Ocean and came to rest off the coast of Africa on the island we now know as Madagascar. When they discovered it, Madagascar had more bizarre and precious animal species than any equivalent piece of real estate in the world. Lemurs of all dimensions dominated the landscape. The largest were the size of gorillas and wandered the lowland forests in company with baboon-sized ground-dwellers and strange, tree-clinging koala-like species as big as Labrador dogs. A lemur the size of a gorilla seems to be an impossibility, yet Julius Caesar could have encountered one had he travelled to Madagascar.

Other, even stranger creatures roamed this abundant isle, among them a termite-eating, aardvark-like creature belonging to a unique order of mammals, the Bibymalagasia. To give an idea of what level of distinctness an order represents, it is well to remember that all primates—from the tiny mouse-lemur to ourselves—comprise an order, as do all of the ruminant animals. Rhinos, horses and tapirs form another. Needless to say, the loss of such a distinctive life form was a severe blow to the planet's biodiversity.

Many other kinds of mammals were also present on Madagascar, as were some astonishing reptiles and birds, such as huge land tortoises and the famed elephant birds. These were, along with a ten-million-year-old giant from Australia, the largest birds ever to stalk the planet. Their eggs still amaze museum-goers around the world. So much was lost from Madagascar 1500 years ago that to a palaeontologist its surviving fauna seems puny and dull.

Five hundred years ago there was still a scattering of islands which had not been pillaged by humanity, and which retained faunas that were a faint echo of this grand world. The very last moa may have trudged the snows of New Zealand's highest peaks at that time, the colossal Steller's sea cow still crawled through the shallows off Bering Island, and the dodo—almost the last of the flightless, gigantic island birds—still flourished on Mauritius. That was all to change, however, as Europe was gripped by a new spirit of adventure.

Columbus' bold undertaking of 1492 opened a new world to Europe. The islands of the Caribbean were the first to feel the impact, and much of the fauna that had survived colonisation by the Indians soon succumbed to hunting or to competition with the rats, pigs and other creatures the Spaniards carried with them. Many species, such as the putative macaws of Hispaniola and curious nesophontine insectivores, vanished even before an adequate description was made of them. Many of the native rodents, such as hutias and rice rats, did not merit the briefest description by the Spanish chroniclers, and all that is known of them must be learned from bones dug up in old refuse dumps or caves. A few species, however, such as the Cuban red macaw and the Little Swan Island hutia, survived long enough for a couple of museum specimens to be secured, and for a few observations of living individuals to be made. Even today a handful of unique Caribbean species, such as the giant shrew-like solenodons of Hispaniola and Cuba, and the tube-nosed nightjar of Hispaniola, hold on; but they are gravely imperilled and far too little is being done to save these last remnants.

Columbus' great achievement galvanised other European powers into venturing on voyages of exploration. By 1500 the Portuguese had encountered Mauritius, the largest non-Arctic island to remain unmolested by humans. It was not settled until the Dutch established their base there in 1598, and within a century the dodo was gone. Thankfully, though, people were beginning to take a greater interest in the creatures they encountered on their travels. We owe our current appreciation of the dodo to a couple of Dutch portraits and to some scattered writings. Nonetheless, a large number of other birds found only on Mauritius or nearby islands—including flightless parrots with giant beaks, red 'hens' with feathers like hair, and snow-white solitaires—all vanished without a museum specimen ever being collected or an accurate, well-provenanced drawing being made. Indeed, even Oxford's famous dodo was not valued as highly as it might have been. It was consigned to a bonfire in 1755 after it began to moulder away. Someone rescued the head and a leg from the flames, and these are now the most solid testimony the world has that this bizarre bird ever existed.

One of the saddest and strangest of stories about a fauna that slipped away without being adequately documented comes from the Mascarene island of Rodrigues. The first humans to live there were eleven French Huguenots who had been driven from their homes in France by religious persecution and marooned on the island in 1691. François Leguat published an account of their adventures in 1708, and for centuries his description of the birds living there was disbelieved as a voyager's fable. Recent investigation of fossil bones found on the island, however, confirms aspects of Leguat's narrative.

Among the strangest of the birds he described was a creature he called the solitary. They were evidently large, upright birds related to dodos, but much more graceful. They could not fly, were monogamous, keenly defended their nests, and raised their single young with great affection. Leguat described some strange behaviours upon fledging:

> some days after the young one leaves the nest, a company of thirty or forty brings another young one to it; and the new fledg'd bird with its father and mother joyning the band, march to some bye place. We frequently followed them, and found that afterwards the old ones went each their way alone, or in couples, and left the two young ones together, which we called a marriage.

His description of the appearance of the bird is also at times a little difficult to comprehend. He mentions bony knobs like musket balls on the wings, and traces of these are preserved in the fossils. When he comes to the feathers, however, things seem even odder. He notes that 'they have two elevations upon the crop, of which the feathers are whiter than the rest, and which resemble, very marvellously, the beautiful bosom of a woman'.

You might have guessed by now that all eleven castaways were men, and that while food, water and shelter were abundant in this island paradise, there was no hope of human female company. In the end desperation drove the Huguenots to build a boat and undertake a perilous voyage across several hundred kilometres of open sea to Mauritius. By the time a natural historian arrived on Rodrigues to check whether the bosom of the solitary really did resemble that of a human female, the birds were all gone. For all its peculiarities, Leguat's account is the most detailed evidence we have of a whole vanished fauna.

By the end of the nineteenth century almost all of the world's virgin islands had been despoiled. Even the remote Bonins, Lord Howe and Christmas, all of which somehow escaped the Polynesian expansion, had been settled and blitzed. An island had to be as tiny, remote and inhospitable as the Indian Ocean's Aldabra to survive, yet such places held little diversity. And the relentless pattern of extinction continued. Now old lands—those already impoverished by people—were being colonised by Europeans, who were precipitating a second tidal wave of extinctions.

Awful cataclysms of extinction overwhelmed the most isolated islands. Hawaii and New Zealand bore the brunt, for each was home to spectacular biodiversity that had escaped earlier human disturbance. In both places the introduction of black and brown rats, along with cats and other predators, was to have a profound impact. A single cat exterminated a whole genus of unique New Zealand birds, while rats carried off species by the dozen. By this time biologists were taking an active interest in the strange island faunas, but their attention was more often than not detrimental, and a number of species appear to have been hunted into extinction by collectors anxious to possess that last skin of a vanishing form. It remains true, however, that we would know very little indeed about many species, and may not have even become aware of the existence of others, were it not for the work undertaken by such collectors.

Lord Walter Rothschild played a larger role in collecting and documenting the world's vanishing creatures than anyone else. He organised and financed expeditions to remote corners of the globe in pursuit of the very rarest species, and his collectors such as Henry Palmer and Albert Meek were often the last people to document a living example of a now extinct species. On occasion they may just have killed the last living individual too.

Born in 1868, Rothschild was a scion of the great banking family and a recipient of the Balfour Declaration, but his greatest love was his museum, which was housed in Hertfordshire at Tring, the family estate. He was a true eccentric, never marrying and never (despite his 191 centimetres and 160 kilograms) moving out of the mansion's nursery wing with its miniature children's furniture. Chronically shy, he spoke either in a hoarse whisper or a loud bellow. Using the family fortune he amassed the greatest natural history collection ever held in private hands, but lost it all to a black-mailing peeress with whom he had a brief affair. He sold his collection to keep her from passing on news of the affair to his mother Emma, whom he feared would be killed by the shock. She lived to be ninety-one.

As technology, and particularly firearms, improved, even the continents proved insufficient refuges for some species. Africa experienced its first extinctions in tens of millennia when the magnificent bluebuck, a relative of the roan and sable antelopes, vanished from the sweet veldt of the Cape around 1800. It was followed a century later and at the opposite extremity of the continent by the red gazelle, while various subspecies such as the quagga, Cape lion and Cape black rhino became extinct around the same period.

Australia was also to experience a renewed cascade of extinction—the first in 46,000 years to blight the land—and it would literally decimate the island continent, carrying off one in every ten of Australia's unique mammal species. This time it was mostly the smaller species that were affected as sheep, cattle and changed burning practices modified the flora, and foxes and cats stalked the land. Curiously Australia's native rodents—descendants of rats and mice which had arrived from Asia around four million years earlier—fared worse than its marsupials, with nine species in all disappearing. Among the marsupials it was the abundant wallabies and bandicoots that suffered most, and today entire tracts of the continent lack these formerly ubiquitous creatures.

A few of Australia's larger marsupials were actively hunted into extinction. The magnificent thylacine, the largest flesh-eating marsupial to survive into the modern age, became extinct in Tasmania in 1936. A bounty was paid on its scalp until the year of its demise. Likewise the toolache wallaby—the swiftest of them all—was hunted into oblivion for pelts and sport by 1939.

Even North America was not vast enough to provide safe refuge to all of its inhabitants. The continent was once home to two of the most breathtaking spectacles nature offered. Its 60 million buffalo roamed the plains in herds a million or more strong. In the nineteenth century, as such a herd passed by, more massed kilograms of a single species were streaming before you than could be seen anywhere else on the planet. North America's passenger pigeon provided an airborne equivalent. So abundant was this bird at the time of European settlement that as the flocks flew overhead they would darken the sun. Their droppings fell as thickly as snow. When they roosted they would occupy stretches of forest 160 kilometres long, perching so densely on branches that their weight sent whole limbs crashing to the ground. Both buffalo and pigeon congregated in

such numbers in order to foil predators. It was a tactic that had worked time out of hand until the Europeans arrived with their new guns. By 1890 both species were in a tailspin towards extinction. Armed guards saved the last buffalo, but nothing effective was done for the pigeon.

There is a biological convention stating that, except in highly unusual circumstances, a species is not proclaimed extinct until fifty years after the last reliable sighting. We have included a large handful of species in this book which have been recorded in the last five decades where there is broad agreement that their extinction is definite. Many other species are probably already lost but have not yet been officially proclaimed so. Their names will eventually appear on the list held by the International Union for the Conservation of Nature in Switzerland.

The last half-century has been marked by an intensifying effort to save the planet's biodiversity, but species by the hundred continue to slip quietly into oblivion. Indeed many scientists would argue that, as the human population builds, the wave of extinctions is gathering momentum. As we worked on this book, another dozen species of birds were officially proclaimed extinct, among them the wonderful glaucous macaw (*Anodorhynchus glaucus*), North America's largest woodpecker, the ivory-bill (*Campephilus principalis*) and the Aldabra bush-warbler (*Nesillas aldabrana*).

China's bizarre Yangtze River dolphin, with its white skin, slender beak and reduced eyes, is down to a single individual, and when it passes away another name will be added to the death list. The world's frogs are now under severe threat, and hundreds if not thousands of species of freshwater fish are extinct or in severe decline. As the planet's rainforests are felled it seems likely that many species as yet undocumented will become extinct, for even large mammals are occasionally discovered in such places. Nor are the oceans immune. Factory ships and trawlers vacuum them for fish, and in 1999 news was first published that a marine fish, the barn-door skate, had been driven to the brink of extinction by such activities.

•

W e have had to be selective in *A Gap in Nature*, concentrating upon birds, mammals and reptiles which are sufficiently well-known for an anatomically accurate drawing to be made of them. The tragedy is that many intriguing species vanished in the three centuries after 1500 without a specimen being collected or a drawing made. Most of the animals in these pages were last seen in the nineteenth and early twentieth centuries, when natural historians were travelling the world, documenting the flora and fauna of remote regions.

These species represent the tip of the extinction iceberg. We deal with only the most obvious of the vertebrates, ignoring all frogs, fish, invertebrates and plants known to have vanished in recent times. When considering whether a species should be included in this book, we resorted to four principal criteria:

It must be a mammal, bird or reptile whose extinction occurred between 1500 and 1999;
It must be known from material sufficiently adequate to allow accurate illustration to be made;
It must be accepted that the organism in question represents a full species, not a subspecies;
It must be widely accepted that the species is extinct.

One hundred and three species were identified that fit these criteria. Sometimes the decision to exclude or include was difficult. For birds, the question of whether a population represents a full species or merely a subspecies was often a vexed one, and impossible to test adequately in extinct forms. Some of our more controversial decisions include the recognition of the Seychelles parakeet and the lesser koa finch as full species, for both have been regarded as mere subspecies or variants by some authors. This problem arose for mammals as well and the celebrated quagga (*Equus quagga quagga*) has been excluded because recent studies reveal it to be a subspecies of Burchell's zebra (*E. q. burchelli*). It, incidentally, represents one of the truly happy endings for extinct forms. Scientists in South Africa are now selectively breeding Burchell's zebras, and quaggas (or creatures very like them) can once again be seen grazing the slopes of Table Mountain near Cape Town. Unfortunately, for all the talk of bringing back extinct species using ancient DNA, such 'resurrections' are not possible once an entire species has been lost.

Many species were excluded for lack of adequate material upon which to base an accurate drawing. Thus, for example, despite being highly distinctive and intriguing, Australia's central hare-wallaby (*Lagorchestes asomatus*) was excluded as it is known only from a single skull and some very general descriptions by Aborigines. So too was the broad-billed parrot (*Lophopsittacus mauritianus*) of the Mascarenes, of which we have only a sketch, a brief description and some fossil remains. The dodo, however, has been included, since a painting, several accurate drawings, descriptions and a mummified head and leg provide sufficient information. The question of knowing that a species is extinct has been most problematic for small mammals and reptiles. The New Guinea long-eared bat (*Pharotis imogene*) has been excluded despite not having been reliably seen since 1891, as has the Jamaican giant galliwasp (*Celestus occiduus*), unsighted since the early nineteenth century. The possibility exists that remnant populations of both species survive.

Given the complexity of the issues involved, and the uncertainty of much information, any such selection will prove unsatisfactory to some. A list of excluded species is provided in the Appendix.

A Gap in Nature

1500

Upland Moa

(Megalapteryx didinus)

Last Record: Subfossil, Surviving to about 1500. Distribution: Subalpine and Alpine Habitats, South Island, New Zealand.

The first Maori arrived in Aotearoa, the archipelago now called New Zealand, around 1200, and in the next few centuries all of its eleven species of moa were hunted to extinction. The upland moa was probably the last to succumb, both because of its remote and inhospitable habitat, and because of its relatively small size. Moa sightings are still occasionally reported, but a large question mark hangs over all historic sightings.

The upland moa appears to have survived until at least 1500 and, although it was never seen by a European, may even have trod the snows of Aotearoa until 1642, the year Abel Tasman discovered the islands. Its remote habitat in the mountainous south is certainly conducive to survival, for the takahe, a large flightless relative of the swamphen, survived in rugged Fiordland in the South Island's far south-west for centuries after it became extinct elsewhere, and was only rediscovered in 1948.

Standing less than a metre high and weighing between seventeen and thirty-four kilograms, the upland moa was small by moa standards. Because of the discovery of several mummified bodies over the last century in dry, cold caves in the Otago area, it is by far the best known of the moas. The mummies reveal that brownish feathers covered the entire body, except for the beak and soles of the feet. Its relatively long, feathered toes may have enabled it to walk on soft snow. Nesting sites have also been found among the rocky crags, some still containing egg fragments. As with the emu and ostrich, the male probably cared for the young, though it differed from those species in brooding just one or a few eggs at a time. It was a herbivore, browsing on alpine shrubs and taking fruits, seeds and berries.

1681
Dodo
(Raphus cucullatus)

Last Record: about 1681. Distribution: Mauritius, Mascarenes.

Fossils reveal that many of the world's islands once supported bizarre birds. Almost all of the most outlandish species were exterminated by native peoples before any historic record could be made. Just one significant subtropical island archipelago retained its full fauna until after 1500—the Mascarene Islands (Mauritius, Réunion and Rodrigues). Their most peculiar inhabitant was doubtless the dodo of Mauritius. By the time of its discovery the bird was thus a strange relict—a reminder of lost worlds that the modern age missed seeing by a whisker of time.

Although it was known to Europeans as a living bird for fewer than ninety years, the dodo had an enormous impact upon their imagination and it became the stuff of stories and folk wisdom. 'As dead as a dodo' remains a byword for something that is truly defunct.

Just what dodos looked like is still debated; some writers describe them as being so fat that their swollen bodies wobbled like jellies as they were chased, their bottoms dragging along the ground; others recalled more slender birds. One observer opined that the dodo might:

> for shape and rareness…antagonise the Phoenix of Arabia; her body is round and fat, few weigh less than 50 pounds…her visage darts forth melancholy, as sensible of nature's injurie in framing so great a body to be guided with complemental wings, so small and impotent, that they serve only to prove her bird…The half of her head is naked seeming covered with a fine vaile, her bill is crooked downwards, in midst is the trill, from which part to the end tis of a light green, mixt with pale yellow tincture; her eyes are small and like to diamonds, round and rowling; her clothing downy feathers, her traine three small plumes, short and improportionable, her legs suiting to her body, her pounces sharp, her appetite strong and greedy.

Scientists argued for centuries about what kind of bird the dodo might be, until anatomical studies decided the point: it was a member of the pigeon family. Indeed it was the largest pigeon species ever to have lived. Despite the sensation of its discovery, little was recorded of its habits in the wild. One writer said it laid a single, white egg in a nest of grass located deep in forest; another that it swallowed stones to aid digestion. Beyond that, its biology is a mystery.

The last complete dodo specimen was held by the Ashmolean Museum at Oxford. In 1755, the ageing mounted skin was ordered out for destruction, but somebody had the foresight to cut off the head and right foot before consigning the rest to the flames, and these are the most substantial dodo remains we have today.

Dodos were ground-nesting birds, and the introduction of monkeys and pigs to Mauritius must have affected their ability to raise young. This, combined with hunting of adults by humans, was sufficient to precipitate their swift decline.

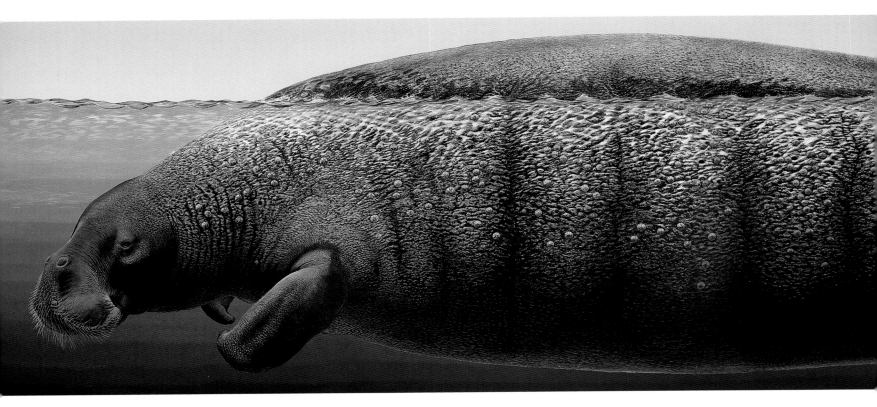

Steller's Sea Cow

(Hydrodamalis gigas)

Last Record: 1768. Distribution: Prehistorically, around the Rim of the North Pacific, from Japan to at least Monterey Bay, California; Historically, Bering and Copper Islands, Commander Group, Western Bering Sea.

With the exception of the great whales, Steller's sea cow was the biggest mammal to survive to modern times. The largest specimens, probably females, could reach over eight metres in length and weigh ten tonnes. Before about 13,000 years ago it was a common and widespread species throughout the coastal regions of the North Pacific. Hunting by Indians and other indigenous people, however, exterminated it and other ice-age giants such as mammoth from the mainland coasts. By two thousand years ago it survived only around the uninhabited Commander Islands in the Bering Sea.

A relative of the dugong, it had a thick, bark-like and uneven skin. Its forelimbs were reduced, having no hand bones. They were curiously bent and were covered on the inside with bristles. Its body was itself an island to smaller creatures such as the barnacles that crusted its sides, while certain fish and seabirds used it as a convenient resting place. Some of its inhabitants, including several species of crustaceans that burrowed deep into its skin, forcing it to ooze a thin serum, were found nowhere else.

All that we know of Steller's sea cow as a living animal comes from the writings of Georg Steller, the naturalist on the Bering Expedition. The expedition had been sent from St Petersburg to explore the far

east, but was shipwrecked on the then unknown Commander Islands in 1741. When the shipwrecked expeditioners discovered the great creatures they were quite numerous in the shallow bays and inlets. Steller wrote that:

> these animals live in herds together in the sea, males and females usually going with one another, pushing the offspring before them all around the shore. These animals are busy with nothing but their food. The back and half the belly are constantly seen outside the water, and they munch along just like land animals with a slow, steady movement forward. With their feet they scrape the seaweed from the rocks, and they masticate incessantly. When the tide recedes, they go from the shore…but with the rising tide they go back again to the beach, often so close that we could reach and hit them with poles. They are not in the least afraid of human beings…they have an extraordinary love for one another, which extends so far that when one of them was cut into, all the others were intent on rescuing it and keeping it from being pulled ashore by closing a circle around it. Others tried to overturn the yawl. Some placed themselves on the rope or tried to draw the harpoon out of its body, in which indeed they were successful several times. We also observed that a male two days in a row came to its dead female on the shore and inquired about its condition…They play the Venus game in June…The female flees—slowly—ahead of the male with constant detours…But when [she] tires of this mock fight and the vain enticements, she lies on her back, and the male completes intercourse in the human way.

Winter was evidently a tough time for these giants. Steller observed that they become so emaciated that not only the ridge of their backbone but every rib showed.

The total population on the Commander Islands probably did not exceed one or two thousand individuals. They were hunted for food, oil and skins, and were extinct within twenty-seven years of their discovery.

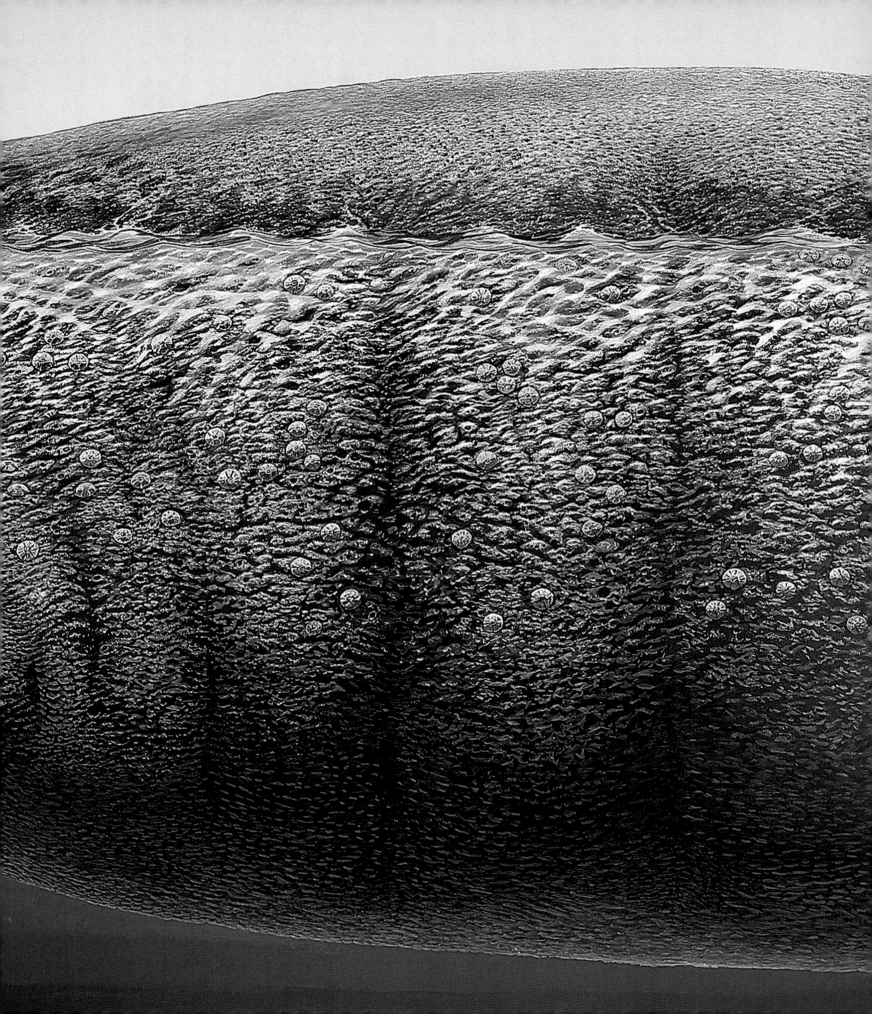

1777

Tahitian Sandpiper

(*Prosobonia leucoptera*)

Last Record: between 12 August and 29 September 1777. Distribution: Tahiti and Moorea, Society Islands.

During his three epic voyages the great navigator James Cook opened a new world to the savants of Europe, but to many of the Pacific islands he visited he brought tragedy in the form of disease, new weapons and pests that triggered a cascade of extinctions. The hardest hit islands seem to have been those that were most welcoming, and in this respect Tahiti reigned supreme.

The Tahitian sandpiper vanished soon after Europeans became aware of it. Its existence was noted by naturalist Johann Forster, who sailed on Cook's second expedition. He found it living close to small brooks and secured a specimen in 1773. Four years later William Anderson, surgeon on Cook's third voyage, found it to be common and collected two more specimens. Yet despite its evident abundance the species has never been heard of since. It seems that Cook was the inadvertent agent of the destruction of these birds. His vessels were plagued with vermin, but at Tahiti during his third expedition things got completely out of hand. Two species of cockroaches were particularly destructive, and the captain wrote, 'If food of any kind was exposed, only for a few minutes, it was covered with them. They were particularly destructive to birds, which had been stuffed and preserved as curiosities…' The roaches were accompanied by rats—probably the brown rat (*Rattus norvegicus*)—and to be rid of them Cook often tied a line from vessel to shore to induce them to jump ship. Some, once they made their tightrope walk to freedom, profited marvellously from Tahiti's unwary birds. Today we have just a single specimen of the Tahitian sandpiper, held by the Naturalis Museum, Leiden, in the Netherlands.

1777

Raiatea Parakeet

(Cyanoramphus ulietanus)

Last Record: between 3 November and 7 December 1777. Distribution: Raiatea, Society Islands.

After an eventful stay at Tahiti, during which he witnessed a human sacrifice, Cook departed on 29 September 1777 to investigate other islands in the group. He headed for nearby Eimeo (now Maiao) Island, where he stayed briefly, and then on to Ulitea (now Raiatea), which lay just a few days sail north-west of Tahiti.

It was during this stopover of thirty-four days on Raiatea that a unique parakeet was collected. At least two individuals were obtained, and today their stuffed skins reside in museums in Vienna and London. Unfortunately, nothing was recorded of the habits of this distinctive bird.

While at Raiatea Cook had the *Resolution* and *Discovery* moored to the shore, and both vessels were heeled and scrubbed. This would have offered a fine opportunity for rats, cockroaches and other vermin to get ashore, and it seems likely that these creatures spelled doom for the Raiatea parakeet.

1788
White Gallinule
(Porphyrio albus)

Last Record: about 1788. Distribution: Lord Howe Island, Australia.

Lord Howe Island was, until 1788, unique in the Pacific Ocean in being a relatively large (1455 hectares), temperate island that had escaped detection by both Polynesian and European explorers. It lies just 570 kilometres off the coast of northern New South Wales, and the first intimation of its existence was a vast cloud of seabirds seen in the area by the French explorer La Perouse. He reported this to members of Australia's First Fleet, who set out in search and sighted the island in March 1788. The place was a convenient larder for the starving convict colony, and in the following years it was systematically plundered.

Among the birds found on the island, all of which were remarkably tame, the stately white gallinule was chicken-sized with a solid red beak and yellowish-red legs. It was clearly a relative of the cosmopolitan purple swamphen, but was flightless, white, and possessed of a more robust bill. Nothing is known of its habits, but given the purple swamphen's propensity to carnivory, it may have been a predator on the chicks of the other bird species that swarmed the island.

Today the white gallinule is sunk in mystery. Just two skins survive, one in Liverpool and one in Vienna, both of which date to the late eighteenth or early nineteenth centuries and are of somewhat uncertain provenance. Some ornithologists dispute that the skins are from Lord Howe Island at all, but historical records confirm that such a bird once existed on the island. One of Lord Howe's earliest visitors was surgeon Arthur Bowes Smythe of the *Lady Penrhyn*, who landed in May 1788. So taken was he with the idyllic, palm-clad island and its utterly tame birds that he wrote 'when I was in the woods amongst the birds I cd. not help picturing to myself the Golden Age as described by Ovid'. Bowes Smythe also wrote of encountering 'fowls or coots some white, some blue and white, others all blue wt. Large red bills'. Some researchers have speculated that the blue birds were purple gallinules (which still exist on the island today), and that the blue-and-white birds were hybrids with the white gallinule. Others, however, consider that all belonged to one variable species.

So little is known of the white gallinule that it is impossible to determine whether it became extinct as early as 1788, or whether it survived until 1834 when the island was first settled. Whatever the case it was clearly gone by 1844. The cause of its demise was almost certainly outright slaughter, for it was not timid and could easily be killed with sticks. It is possible that hybridisation with the purple swamphen may also have played a role. Rats and cats cannot be blamed, for they arrived much later.

Bluebuck

(*Hippotragus leucophaeus*)

Last Record: 1799–1800. Distribution: South-western South Africa.

The bluebuck or blue antelope was a relative of the roan and sable antelopes, but was a little smaller than both. It was probably a selective feeder, preferring high-quality grasses. Fossils indicate that it was more widespread during the last ice age than when first encountered by Europeans in the seventeenth century. It was then restricted to the extreme southern coastal portion of South Africa, and even very early observers report that it was uncommon. It may have been affected by competition from domestic sheep, which reached South Africa around AD 400 after being traded with tribes from the north. Following European settlement its decline became terminal, for despite the fact that its flesh was distasteful it was hunted avidly, and eventually much of its habitat was converted to agriculture. By around 1800 there were none left.

Today just four mounted specimens survive in museums in Vienna, Stockholm, Paris and Leiden, along with some bones and horn sets in other places. All of these museum specimens are now more than two hundred years old, and none shows any trace of the blue colour the creature was reported to possess, and that its common name suggests. Truly blue fur does not occur in mammals, and the bluebuck may have derived its bluish tinge from a mixture of black and yellow hairs. These are the tones Peter Schouten has used in this painting to give a sense of our understanding of the original colouration of this noble animal.

Small Mauritian Flying-fox
(*Pteropus subniger*)

Last Record: Early 1800s. Distribution: Réunion and Mauritius, Mascarenes.

The larger Mascarene islands once supported two species of flying-fox. Both were unique to the group, and were quite different in appearance and habits. The larger species, known as the Mauritian flying-fox, still survives, though in reduced numbers. In many ways it is a typical flying-fox, similar to those still to be seen throughout much of Asia and Australasia today. The smaller species, however, known as the small Mauritian flying-fox, was evidently quite different.

The small Mauritian flying-fox was once abundant. Early observers record that up to four hundred would crowd together at a single roost in a cave or in an ancient, hollow tree. Both roosting places are unusual for flying-foxes, which prefer the branches of large trees. Locals believed that no matter how large the roost, only one male would be present. This may indicate that the sexes roosted separately, and that perhaps the large roosts were maternity colonies. It was strictly nocturnal in its habits and its delicate teeth indicate that it probably fed upon nectar and possibly soft fruit.

Its habit of roosting *en masse* in old trees and caves may have left it vulnerable to both forest clearance and hunting. In any case, it appears to have vanished well before the close of the nineteenth century. The effect of its extinction on the Mascarene forests remains unknown, but one wonders whether it was the sole pollinator or agent of dispersal for any long extinct plant species. Specimens still exist in museums in Paris, London, Berlin and Sydney.

1825

Mysterious Starling

(Aplonis mavornata)

Last Record: Early Afternoon, 9 August 1825. Distribution: Mauke, Cook Islands.

For over a century the mysterious starling was known from a single specimen. It was clearly a distinct species, but was accompanied by no information stating when or where it had been collected. Several of the world's most eminent ornithologists travelled to London to examine it, but the bird remained a complete mystery—hence its common name.

Dr Storrs Olson of the Smithsonian Institution solved the riddle in 1986. He located an old and neglected manuscript in the British Museum, numbered M8s BLO, which was an account of a nineteenth century voyage by Mr Andrew Bloxham, naturalist aboard HMS *Blonde*. The vessel sailed under the command of Captain Byron (cousin to the poet), and departed England on 28 September 1824, on a doleful mission. The *Blonde* was bound for Hawaii, to return the bodies of King Liholiho and Queen Kamamalu to their subjects after both had succumbed to measles during a royal visit to England.

The *Blonde* returned home via Cape Horn, and Andrew Bloxham had the opportunity to visit several islands. He was on Mauke for just two hours, and the fact that he was able to collect a specimen of the mysterious starling during such a brief visit suggests that it was then common. Mauke was not visited again by a biologist until the early 1970s, at which time no sign of the species was found. All that is known of it, beyond the ageing skin, is Bloxham's note that the bird was 'killed hopping about a tree'.

1826

Mauritius Blue Pigeon

(*Alectroenas nitidissima*)

Last Record: 1826. Distribution: Mauritius, Mascarenes.

Monsieur Julien Desjardins, who lived all of his life on Mauritius, left us the only eye-witness account of this remarkable species. 'This bird lives alone near the river banks,' he wrote. 'It eats fruit and freshwater molluscs.' The trouble with these snippets, however, is that related species, which survive in Madagascar and the Seychelles, form large flocks and inhabit forests where they feed on fruit. No pigeons are known to eat molluscs, though the strange lives of many island species should warn us off dismissing Desjardins' note out of hand.

This large and beautiful pigeon was avidly hunted, and this may have been the principal cause of its extinction. Vast plagues of rats were also reported on the island during the eighteenth century. Indeed it was reported that a particularly troublesome rat plague drove the Dutch from the island in 1710, after 112 years of occupation. If this were not enough then the introduction of macaques, which are known to be great egg thieves, may have been the final straw for this beautiful bird. Just three specimens exist, all held in European museums.

Tongan Giant Skink

(Tachygia microlepis)

Last Record: April–May 1827. Distribution: Tongatapu, Tongan Islands.

The giant skink of Tonga was a magnificent creature that slipped into extinction before anything was known about it except the fact that it existed. Just two specimens survive, both pickled in alcohol in the Muséum National d'Histoire Naturelle, Paris, where they have lain for nearly two centuries. They were collected by naturalists Jean René Quoy and Joseph Paul Gaimard on a voyage round the world with Captain J. S. C. Dumont d'Urville aboard the French corvette *l'Astrolabe* between 1826 and 1829. Dumont d'Urville was a fascinating if tragic figure. He seems to have been the Forrest Gump of his age, always being there at critical moments in history, usually in the company of the famous. One of his more memorable exploits was the discovery of the Venus de Milo. He was one of the few people to see her with arms, which were shortly afterwards lost in a tussle between French sailors and Greek brigands. He was also the only explorer from the days of sail to die in a train crash. After surviving extreme vicissitudes at the ends of the earth he perished during a family outing to Versailles on a sunny day in early May 1842.

The Tongan giant skink, shown here at life-size, were collected under the most trying of circumstances. During most of the *Astrolabe's* month-long stay in the Tongan Islands she was in imminent danger of shipwreck, having sailed too close to a reef on a lee shore. Dumont d'Urville paints a vivid picture of Quoy's activities at the expedition's moment of greatest crisis, when the *Astrolabe's* bow lay just three metres from the jagged coral, and was pitching so violently in the huge swell that her lower spars seemed to touch the menacing foam. Quoy's table was set up on the quarterdeck, Dumont d'Urville wrote, where the scientist:

> went on with his work of analysis and natural history drawings…and to see him calmly working away, one would have never guessed that at any moment *Astrolabe* could sink, leaving those on board only time to jump for their lives…I encouraged him as best I could, pretending an interest in his research which at that moment I was incapable of feeling. But it was a way of hiding from the sailors the full extent of the danger that was threatening them.

The skinks were probably brought aboard by visiting Tongans, who traded with the naturalists through the worst of their peril. Perhaps Dumont d'Urville's pretended interest extended as far as the giant skink. If so he was one of just a handful of Europeans to see a fresh or living specimen. The timing and cause of their extinction is entirely unknown.

PETER SCHOUTEN 00

1828

Kosrae Starling

(Aplonis corvina)

Last Record: between December 1827 and January 1828. Distribution: Kosrae, Caroline Islands.

Between 1826 and 1829 the German biologist and explorer Friedrich von Kittlitz assembled one of the most important biological collections ever made. He travelled as a civilian passenger aboard the Russian vessel *Senjawin*, captained by Friedrich Lüdke, on a voyage around the world, stopping in at many islands before the onset of devastation brought about by European settlement.

While visiting Kosrae Island in Micronesia's Caroline group von Kittlitz encountered a starling which even then he considered to be rare. It was an inhabitant of mountain forests, and as its scientific name suggests it was a crow-like bird that, at twenty centimetres long, was remarkably large for a member of the starling genus. The repeated introduction of rats from whaling vessels that were careened on the island was almost certainly the principal factor in its decline. Subsequent searches of the rugged and mountainous island, the first by German biologist and explorer Otto Finsch in 1881, failed to record it. The only known specimens of this unique creature are held in the Leningrad Museum.

1828

Kosrae Crake

(*Porzana monasa*)

Last Record: between December 1827 and January 1828. Distribution: Kosrae, Caroline Islands.

The Kosrae crake was a fairly large, dark-coloured and possibly flightless member of the rail family. Just two examples now remain, both held in St Petersburg, and both collected by von Kittlitz in marshes at sea level. Even in von Kittlitz's time the species appears to have been uncommon.

Long after its extinction the bird's habits were recalled by the people of Kosrae, who related what they remembered to members of the Whitney South Seas Expedition, when they visited the island in 1931. The islanders called it the *nay-tai-mai-not*, meaning 'to land in the taro garden'. W. F. Coultas, who participated in the expedition, wrote:

> In the olden days it was a sacred bird, but since the Christian missions have been established not much attention has been paid to older faiths…Several oldsters seem to remember their forefathers' speaking of the bird, but none of them admitted having seen it, except an elderly Deacon, a staunch pillar of the Church, who claimed to have had it pointed out to him twenty years previous to my visit.

When Otto Finsch visited Kosrae in 1881 he found the place overrun with rats, but neither saw nor heard any sign of the crake. The rats—presumably black rats (*Rattus rattus*)—were still in plague proportions fifty years later when Coultas visited, and they may well have been the principal cause of the birds' decline.

1828

Kittlitz's Thrush

(Zoothera terrestris)

Last Record: 1828. Distribution: Peel (Chichijima) Island, Ogasawara (Bonin) Archipelago, Japan.

After visiting Kosrae the *Senjawin* set sail for the Bonin Islands, a volcanic archipelago lying in what is now southern Japanese waters. There, von Kittlitz was destined to find even more natural treasures, making his greatest discoveries on Peel Island, where he collected four specimens of a medium-sized and rather undistinguished-looking ground thrush. In 1828 the island was still in a near virginal state, its total human population consisting of just two castaways—and they were the only humans ever to have set foot on the island.

Just a few months after von Kittlitz departed, however, HMS *Blossom* arrived, and just three years later English, Americans and Polynesians came ashore and settled. American whaling vessels began visiting the island to careen and repair, and the rats, cats and other mammals they brought with them quickly exterminated Peel Island's ground-dwelling birds.

Von Kittlitz recorded nothing of the habits of this obscure species. Despite the best efforts of several ornithological expeditions that visited Peel between 1889 and 1930, it has not been seen again. Von Kittlitz's collection was originally housed in St Petersburg, but the four specimens of his ground thrush are now dispersed between museums in Frankfurt, St Petersburg, Leiden and Vienna.

1828

Bonin Islands Grosbeak

(Chaunoproctus ferreorostris)

Last Record: 1828. Distribution: Peel (Chichijima) Island, Ogasawara (Bonin) Archipelago, Japan.

In addition to the thrush named after him, Friedrich von Kittlitz was privileged to collect another species on Peel Island that would never be seen by the trained human eye again. The Bonin Islands grosbeak (a kind of finch) vanished into oblivion after his short visit to its homeland in 1828. This bird was, according to von Kittlitz, remarkably tame, as one might expect of a species that had evolved on an island that until about 1827 had no human inhabitants. It was a denizen of the forest, where solitary birds or pairs were often seen on the ground searching for buds and fruits. Its call was a 'soft, pure, high piping note, given sometimes shorter, sometimes longer'.

Beginning in 1830 goats, sheep, dogs, cats and rats arrived with settlers on the archipelago, and the destruction they wrought on Peel was swift. By 1854, when the American naturalist William Simpson visited the island, no sign of the grosbeak could be found.

1834
Delalande's Coucal
(*Coua delalandei*)

Last Record: 1834. Distribution: Madagascar.

Many museums keep all of their specimens of extinct birds together in a single drawer or cabinet. When I was shown the Philadelphia Academy of Natural Sciences' collection of extinct birds, one specimen stood out from the rest. It was an example of Delalande's coucal, a truly magnificent bird about the size of a raven, with an electric-blue back, white breast and white-tipped tail.

Very little is known about the species, for it disappeared, or at least became exceedingly rare, at an early date. Although a member of the cuckoo family, it brooded its own eggs, and was evidently ground-dwelling. Coucals with similar habits still exist throughout much of the African, Asian and Australian tropics today, but none possesses the vibrant colours of Delalande's coucal.

The species was restricted to wet forest in north-eastern Madagascar, where the last specimen collected by a European was acquired in 1834. It may have survived much longer, however, as there are reports of birds being trapped as late as the 1920s by native hunters in the Fito and Maroantsetra areas. Hunting may have been a significant factor in its decline and extinction, as its beautiful plumes were highly prized.

1834

Mascarene Parrot

(*Mascarinus mascarinus*)

Last Record: 1834. Distribution: Réunion Island, Mascarenes.

For years uncertainty reigned about the original habitat of the Mascarene parrot. Some thought it was originally an inhabitant of Madagascar, others the Mascarenes. The definitive evidence came to light in 1893, when an English translation of a long-neglected French manuscript was published by the Hakluyt Society. In this work Sieur Bubois described his voyages to the Mascarene Islands between 1669 and 1692. He mentions that on Réunion there lived 'parrots a little larger than pigeons, having plumage of greyish colour, a black hood on the head, the beak very large, & the colour of fire'. The description fits the Mascarene parrot precisely, and is the best evidence we have about the original home of this species.

Just two specimens exist in museum collections today, both obtained during the opening years of the nineteenth century. The last known living individual was held in the zoological collection of the King of Bavaria, where it survived until at least 1834, long after the wild population had vanished. The precise cause of the bird's extinction is unknown.

1837

Oahu 'O'o

(Moho apicalis)

Last Record: 1837. Distribution: Oahu, Hawaiian Islands.

The Hawaiian Islands were once home to a rich variety of birds, whose ancestors must have traversed vast expanses of ocean to reach the isolated isles. Few, perhaps, hail from so distant a shore as the 'o'os, a group belonging to the Australian honeyeater family, Meliphagidae. Perhaps blown by winds or cyclones across thousands of kilometres of empty ocean, their landfall on distant Hawaii seems to have been a one-in-a-million chance. Fate was not to be so kind, however, following European contact.

The Oahu 'o'o may have been collected by Europeans on as few as two occasions, and all that remains of the species today is half a dozen specimens scattered throughout European and North American museums. The first specimen brought to Europe arrived with the *Blonde*, which had visited the island carrying the bodies of King Liholiho and his Queen Kamamalu, who had died on their royal tour of England. Twelve years later a German at Honolulu, Herr Deppe, collected a number of specimens in the hills behind the town. A couple of other skins, whose provenance is unknown, but which may have been collected at the same time, exist in museum drawers. Nothing was recorded of the habits of this first 'o'o to suffer extinction before it slipped into oblivion.

1840

Huppe

(Fregilupus varius)

Last Record: between 1835 and 1840. Distribution: Réunion Island, Mascarenes.

Starlings are great colonisers, and many islands once had their own distinct species, evolved from ancestors that arrived in the remote past. None was so peculiar as the huppe of Réunion Island, whose most distinctive feature was described by one ornithologist as a 'crest of pale, decomposed feathers'. Like many island birds, the huppe appears to have been remarkably unafraid of humans, and could even be knocked down with sticks. One resident wrote:

> their song was a clear note [and they were] very tame and, being young, I killed dozens of them. When I returned to the island after ten years in Paris, I found no further trace of them. I used to keep them in a cage without any trouble. They eat bananas, potatoes, cabbage etc.

The story is almost a parable of human interaction with vanished species, in which a carefree youth kills thoughtlessly, only to repent in maturity the loss of such magnificent creatures.

The final cause of the huppe's demise may have been the introduction of rats and, given the above, their decline to extinction may have been swift. Given their adaptability to life with humans, it is a great pity that a captive population was not established.

1843
Big-eared Hopping-mouse
(Notomys macrotis)

Last Record: 19 July 1843. Distribution: Moore River Area, South-western Australia.

Australia is home to a great diversity of native rats and mice. Indeed this group makes up around one-quarter of the continent's mammal fauna. Unfortunately they have suffered even greater rates of extinction since European colonisation than have the continent's marsupials, and no group suffered more severely than the hopping-mice. Inhabitants of the inland plains, and with many species having quite restricted distributions, they were vulnerable to the advent of agriculture and pastoralism, as well as to introduced predators such as cats and foxes.

The hopping-mice somewhat resemble miniature kangaroos, and move by bounding upon their enlarged hind feet. The big-eared hopping-mouse was a small rat-sized species, known from just two damaged specimens held in the Natural History Museum, London. At least one of these was taken by collector John Gilbert in July 1843, while in the employ of the great wildlife artist John Gould. Within two years of collecting this specimen Gilbert would be dead, having been speared by Aborigines during Leichhardt's famous expedition from Brisbane to Port Essington in the top end of Australia.

It was possibly the first of the Australian mammals to succumb to European-wrought changes in the environment. Nothing is known of the biology of the species, but it appears to have been related to the fawn hopping-mouse, which survives in central Australia.

1844

Tahiti Parakeet

(Cyanoramphus zealandicus)

Last Record: 1844. Distribution: Tahiti, Society Islands.

The Tahiti parakeet was known as the *a'a* to the natives of Tahiti. It belongs to a genus that today has its distribution centred on New Zealand. In the past, however, it was far more widespread in the Pacific.

The first European to record the Tahiti parakeet was the artist Sydney Parkinson, who sailed in 1768 with James Cook and Sir Joseph Banks in the *Endeavour*. He made a drawing of the bird but did not live to report his find, dying on 27 January 1771 of dysentery, which he contracted when the vessel stopped at Batavia, then a notoriously disease-ridden port. The fate of the specimen from which the drawing was made is unclear, but other specimens were collected on subsequent Cook expeditions that touched at Tahiti, and it is probably from these voyages that three of the four known specimens held in museums today originate.

The very last record is of a specimen collected by Lieutenant de Marolles, who visited Tahiti in 1844. Three birds were taken, one of which arrived as a skin at the Muséum National d'Histoire Naturelle, Paris. The fate of the others is unknown. As with the Raiatea parakeet, the introduction of rats, and possibly cats, may have been decisive factors in its extinction.

1844

Great Auk

(Pinguinus impennis)

Last Record: 3 June 1844. Distribution: North Atlantic, Breeding on Bird Rocks (Gulf of St Lawrence), Funk Island (off Newfoundland), Grimsey, the Geirfulasker and Eldey (all off Iceland) and St Kilda (the westernmost Hebrides).

With the exception of the dodo, the great auk is perhaps the best known of all recently extinct species. It was the bird to which the name penguin was originally applied, and it resembled the penguins of the southern oceans in both body shape and lifestyle. Fossilised bones of the great auk have been found over a vast area around the North Atlantic. As human numbers grew, however, it retreated to remote islands to breed, and by the beginning of the sixteenth century its colonies were few and scattered. The great auk was a stately bird far larger than any of its relatives and a powerful swimmer. It was awkward on land, but at home in the ocean, where it presumably chased fish, crustaceans and cephalopods much as the penguins still do. Its gape was bright yellow, and the only noise it was ever heard to utter was 'a few low croaks'. It laid its rather pear-shaped egg directly onto the rocks,—the shape was important in preventing the egg from rolling away.

While at sea the great auk was safe from human assault, but at its nest it was exquisitely vulnerable. It had been hunted since prehistoric times by fishermen and fowlers, but with the European expansion it came under increasingly serious assault. In 1534 the French explorer Jacques Cartier discovered its greatest redoubt, Funk Island off north-east Newfoundland. He and subsequent explorers provisioned their ships at the teeming colony. They were followed by cod fishermen and lobster catchers, who used auk as bait. At this time they were so common that people filled boats with the animal's carcasess.

By the early nineteenth century the great auk only came ashore regularly on some islands off Iceland. Its few encounters with humans after this date comprise, as the biographer of extinct birds Errol Fuller puts it, 'a squalid list of human ignorance and cruelty'. One of the last auks to visit St Kilda was captured live. It was caged and a few nights later there were strong winds. The next morning it was beaten to death by the islanders, who were by now so unfamiliar with the stately, upright bird that they believed it might be a witch!

The birds last stronghold was known as the Geirfulasker for the 'geirfugl' or great auks that nested there. This rocky stack off the Iceland coast was a fuming volcano. In 1830 the Geirfulasker, in a paroxysm of activity, sank beneath the waves. The few surviving birds had just one refuge left, the nearby island of Eldey. There, on 3 June 1844, a party of sailors landed, having been sent by a collector to check if any great auks remained. They spotted a pair, standing head and shoulders above the masses of smaller seabirds. Legend has it that the female was brooding an egg, a last hope for the future of the magnificent birds.

The great auks made a desperate attempt to reach the safety of the water, but one was trapped between some rocks, while the other was seized just a few metres from the edge of the sea. Both were clubbed to death. The egg, it is believed, was crushed beneath a sailor's boot. Some eighty skins and seventy-five eggs held in museum collections of the world are all that remain of the great auk today.

1845
White-footed Rabbit-rat

(Conilurus albipes)

Last Record: 1845. Distribution: South-eastern Australia.

The white-footed rabbit-rat, about the size of a kitten, was one of Australia's most beautiful and largest native rodents. It was once found from Adelaide to Sydney. An illustration of it was executed by a First Fleet artist shortly after 1788. The Sydney natives called it *gnar-ruck*, and although it was common enough to be a problem in the settler's stores, it was never recorded again in the Sydney area.

It lived in woodlands, and made nests filled with leaves and possibly grass in the limbs of hollow eucalypts. The collector John Gould stated that it was nowhere common, and that it was strictly nocturnal. Its young were carried attached to the mother's teats. Sir George Grey, while governor of South Australia, wrote to John Gould:

> This animal lives among the trees. The specimen I send you, a female, had three young ones attached to its teats when it was caught…while life remained in the mother they remained attached to her teats by their mouths…On pulling the young from the teats of the dead mother, they seized hold of my glove with the mouth and held on so strongly it was difficult to disengage them.

The last authenticated record of the species is from South Australia, and was made in or before 1845. The catalogue of the Blandowski Expedition, sent from the Museum of Victoria to the junction of the Murray and Darling rivers in 1856–57, states four specimens were collected, but these have been lost and the identification is doubtful. In the 1980s Mr Norman Maher, from the Deniliquin area of southern New South Wales told me that he sometimes saw a creature closely resembling the white-footed rabbit-rat a few miles north of town during the 1930s.

The disappearance of this relatively widespread species soon after settlement is intriguing. Rats—brown in Sydney, brown or black in South Australia—may have transmitted a disease or competed directly with the white-footed rabbit-rat. Cats were also predators. Many argue that Aboriginal firestick farming maintained the woodland inhabited by this species, and it is possible that the cessation of this traditional practice doomed both the white-footed rabbit-rat and its habitat.

1850

Spectacled Cormorant

(Phalacrocorax perspicillatus)

Last Record: about 1850. Distribution: Bering and Commander Islands, North Pacific.

The spectacled cormorant was a huge, apparently flightless bird restricted to a few uninhabited islands in the northern Pacific. It was first encountered by members of the Bering expedition, who had travelled from Siberia to Alaska and become stranded, in November 1741.

Georg Steller, the expedition's zoologist, recorded a very large cormorant with white markings around its eyes, but did not live to bring news of his discovery to Europe. After escaping Bering Island on a makeshift vessel, he wandered through Siberia for four years, seeking a way home to St Petersburg before succumbing to the rigours of his travels.

In Steller's day the great cormorants were abundant, and were a staple source of food for the shipwrecked mariners. One bird, which could weigh in excess of seven kilograms, made a good meal for three hungry Russians. In 1826 the Russian–American Company brought a number of Aleut workers to Bering Island to collect seal and sea-otter pelts. They found the bird good to eat, as did the natives of Kamchatka, who cooked it by encasing it in a large lump of clay and placing it over hot coals. The last birds seem to have disappeared into an Aleut cooking pot by 1850.

All specimens of the bird in museums today were collected around a century after Steller's discovery. They were either given as gifts or sold by Governor Kuprianof, who in the 1840s presided over the Sitka district of Siberia, including Bering Island. The ornithologist Dr Leonard Stejneger spent eighteen months in 1882–83 exploring the islands and searching for the species, but was told by the inhabitants that they had not seen it for around thirty years. Its last refuge, they reported, was the islet known as Aij Kamen in the Commander Group.

1851
Norfolk Island Kaka
(*Nestor productus*)

Last Record: about 1851. Distribution: Norfolk Island, Australia.

Norfolk Island is an isolated volcanic peak rising from the ocean floor 1670 kilometres east-north-east of Sydney, Australia. It was settled in 1788 by the British, and a heavy toll was taken of its fauna and flora thereafter. One of the largest land birds on the island was the Norfolk Island kaka, whose nearest relatives are found over 1000 kilometres to the south in New Zealand. Almost nothing is known of the species, except that it was very shy and that its call sounded like a dog barking in the treetops. Several specimens had grossly overgrown upper bills that may have resulted from inbreeding in the small population.

Norfolk Island was settled as a convict colony and faced starvation in its early years. The kaka were large and unwary birds, and a recent manuscript find indicates that hunting had a heavy impact at a surprisingly early date. The journal of American sailor Jacob Nagle, who stayed on the island from March 1790 to February 1791, was only discovered in 1983 and published in 1988. In it he recalls that:

> there was but few land birds on the island eccepting quail, a few parrots [the kaka], parokeets that fed on the wild red peper, and some wild pigeons of the same colour as our tame pigeons, but we reduced them a great deal before we left the island.

If any of the birds survived hunting, habitat destruction would have soon caught up with them, for kaka need hollow trees to nest in, and the settlers quickly cleared the forest. The last known Norfolk Island kaka died in a cage in London around 1851. Kaka were long-lived birds, and the individual may have survived in captivity for many decades. The species was long gone from Norfolk by the time of the captive bird's demise, although local legend has it that a few individuals survived on Phillip Island, an islet just off Norfolk, until the second half of the nineteenth century.

1852

St Lucy Giant Rice-rat

(Megalomys luciae)

Last Record: 1852. Distribution: Santa Lucia, Caribbean.

The islands of the Caribbean were once home to a marvellously rich fauna. The giant rice-rats of some of the Lesser Antilles survived longer than most, but the St Lucy species became extinct some time during the latter half of the nineteenth century. Almost nothing is known about it; the last recorded specimen died in London Zoo in 1852, after having survived in captivity for three years. It differed from its relative the Martinique giant rice-rat in its darker belly and aspects of its skeleton, as well as in its slender, narrow claws.

The only specimen I have seen (possibly the only one in existence) is in the Natural History Museum, London, where it resides in a glass-topped box in a museum drawer surrounded by hundreds of its smaller (still surviving) relatives. Whoever stuffed it did a poor job. The specimen, which is the size of a small cat, is now falling apart and is so fragile it bears a label with a strict injunction not to touch it.

1857

Gould's Mouse

(Pseudomys gouldii)

Last Record: 1856–57. Distribution: Eastern Inland Australia.

Gould's mouse belonged to a group of mouse- and rat-sized native Australian rodents that was abundant at the time of European settlement. The species was named by John Gould for his wife Elizabeth, who was a finer artist than her husband, and whose work was a key element in the success of his books. Gould's mouse was slightly smaller than a black rat (*Rattus rattus*) and was evidently quite social, living in small family groups that sheltered in a burrow during the day. These were usually dug under bushes, and at a depth of around fifteen centimetres the family could be found resting together in a nest of soft dry grass.

Subfossil accumulations of bones indicate that Gould's mouse was common and widespread in the inland regions of eastern Australia prior to settlement. Indeed, it was collected at a number of widely separated localities between the 1830s and 1850s, but thereafter it quickly disappeared, though exactly what changes impacted upon it most severely are unclear. Cats arrived in Australia with the First Fleet, and they may have played a role in exterminating the species. Grazing stock and changed fire regimes may also have played a part, as may competition with introduced rats and mice and introduced diseases. The species certainly vanished before foxes arrived, so they cannot be implicated. The last specimens were collected by members of the Blandowski Expedition, near the junction of the Murray and Darling rivers, in 1856–57. Unfortunately most of the specimens of now extinct species collected during this expedition have vanished. Blandowski, the expedition leader, had a falling-out with the Museum of Victoria, and packed his collection for shipment to Poland. This was the last that was ever heard of them.

1859

Kioea

(Chaetoptila angustipluma)

Last Record: 1859. Distribution: Hawaii and Oahu, Hawaiian Islands.

The kioea was a member of the Australian Meliphagidae, the same family to which the 'o'os belong. It, however, was a far more typical member of the honeyeaters, and perhaps was derived from a separate, more recent colonisation of the islands from faraway Australia. At around thirty centimetres long it was large, greenish in colour and similar in appearance to the larger Australian honeyeaters. Even its call, reported to be a loud 'chuck', is similar to that of Australia's wattle birds. The native Hawaiian name for this species means 'standing high on long legs'.

Fossil evidence indicates that in prehistoric times the kioea was found on a number of the Hawaiian Islands and favoured dry woodland or scrub in the lowlands. Destruction of this habitat, probably through clearing, had made it rare by the time of European contact. Then only a small relict population survived in the mountains of Hawaii, in an area of marginal habitat.

The first Europeans to encounter it were Charles Pickering and Titian R. Peale of the United States Exploring Expedition, who collected it in 1840 on a high plateau near the upper edge of the forest. They wrote that 'it is very active and graceful in its motions, frequents the woody districts, and is disposed to be musical' (which, incidentally, hardly accords with other descriptions of its call).

Two decades after these notes were made a Hawaiian shopkeeper with an interest in birds collected the last known specimens, possibly in the hills above Hilo.

1859

Jamaican Least-pauraqué

(*Siphonorhis americanus*)

Last Record: 1859. Distribution: Jamaica, Caribbean.

The Jamaican least-pauraqué was a peculiar kind of nightjar or goatsucker, distinguishable from its near relatives by its possession of tubular nostrils around two millimetres long. Just what function these strange nostrils performed is entirely unknown. It belongs to a genus unique to the Caribbean that includes just one other species, which still survives on Hispaniola.

Tragically, the Jamaican least-pauraqué was an obscure night bird of which no natural history observations were made, for it slipped into extinction before anything could be learned of it. Only a handful of museum specimens, mostly in the United States and Britain, survive.

Cuban Red Macaw

(Ara tricolor)

Last Record: 1864. Distribution: Cuba, Caribbean.

The Cuban red macaw (following left-hand page) was a pygmy in its genus, just a third the size of its largest South American relatives. Its foods included the fruit of the white cedar *Melia azdarach* (a common street tree in warmer climates today), as well as the fruit of other trees and palms. It was reputed to have nested in holes in palms.

Records from the sixteenth century suggest that it or a very similar species may once have inhabited Hispaniola and even Jamaica, but macaws vanished early from these islands and descriptions are pathetically vague. It must have been widespread on Cuba in the early days of settlement, but it had vanished from most of the island before it became an object of interest to ornithologists in the second half of the nineteenth century. It remained, however, relatively easy to find around Zapata Swamp as late as 1849.

Despite the fact that its flesh was reputed to be evil-smelling and bad to taste, the Cuban red macaw was hunted for meat, and its nests were raided for pets. Early records suggest that it spent most of its time in pairs or small parties, but almost nothing else was recorded of its habits. The last known specimen was shot in the vicinity of Zapata Swamp in 1864, although records suggest that a few individuals survived there until the 1880s. A dozen specimens are held in museums around the world.

1870

Seychelles Parakeet

(*Psittacula wardi*)

Last Record: June 1870. Distribution: Mahé and Silhouette, Seychelles, Indian Ocean.

The downfall of the Seychelles parakeet (following right-hand page) seems to have been a fondness for ripening maize. The species was persecuted by islanders for raiding their crops, and its last stronghold was on Mahé, which is a small, steep island that rises abruptly to around 700 metres above the sea. It survived there until at least 1870, but a search of the island in 1906 failed to reveal it and it has not been seen since. Nothing, except a fondness for maize, was recorded of its habits.

1870

Kawekaweau

(Hoplodactylus delcourti)

Last Record: 1870. Distribution: North Island, New Zealand.

Maori legend has it that a giant lizard, known as the kawekaweau, once inhabited Aotearoa. The last one seen by Maori was caught by a chief of the Urewera tribe, who found it living under the loose bark of a dead tree in the Waimana Valley in 1870. He described it as being as thick as a man's wrist, brownish in colour with red stripes. But no specimen was kept and the kawekaweau came to be considered by biologists as a legendary or fantastical creature.

Then, in 1986, researchers published an article announcing the 'discovery' of an ancient stuffed lizard skin, mounted on a plank, that had lain unrecognised in a museum in Marseilles, France, for well over a century. No one knew how it came to be there, or even when it was collected, for it had no label. The scientists who examined it, however, were amazed by it because it was by far the largest gecko they had ever seen, being half as long again as the largest previously known species. When they analysed it closely they found that it belonged to a genus that was only known from New Zealand, and that faint reddish stripes could be discerned on its back. It was, they surmised, a specimen of the kawekaweau, the only one to have survived to give credence to the old Maori tales.

The kawekaweau has not been recorded as a living creature for over a hundred and thirty years, and it is almost certainly extinct. It must have been an important predator and possible pollinator and herbivore in New Zealand's ecosystem, for large geckoes can have a wide diet. Unfortunately it vanished before anything could be learned of its biology. The causes of its extinction remain unclear, but it seems likely that rats, weasels and cats would have had a negative impact.

1874
Samoan Wood-rail
(*Pareudiastes pacificus*)

Last Record: 1873 or 1874. Distribution: Savaii, Samoan Islands.

The Samoan wood-rail was a small, dark and flightless relative of the moorhen. It was known to Europeans for a remarkably short time: the first specimen came to light in 1869 and the last one five years later. Nevertheless, the interval was sufficient to allow William Pritchard, former British consul to Fiji, to decide that it was 'excellent eating'. The Samoans knew it as *puna'e* and presumably understood its habits well, but little was recorded by western naturalists during the brief period it was available to them.

It was evidently a secretive species, and its large eyes indicate that it may have been crepuscular or nocturnal. It seems to have favoured swamps, and laid its eggs in a rudimentary nest on the ground. Just eleven skins and a single egg survive as testimony to its existence. Rats, cats and other introduced species may have eliminated it.

1874
Large Palau Flying-fox
(Pteropus pilosus)

Last Record: about 1874. Distribution: Palau Islands, Micronesia.

The large Palau flying-fox, which had a wingspan of about sixty centimetres, is known from just two specimens, both collected in the Palau Islands prior to 1874. The earlier specimen now resides in a jar of alcohol in the Natural History Museum, London. It is a sad-looking, brownish creature, the long silvery hairs on its belly that were once one of its most distinctive features are still faintly visible. The skull has been extracted for study, but was badly broken and adds little to our understanding of this individual, except that it was relatively young.

Extensive surveys of the Palau island group, both in 1931 and more recently, have failed to reveal the presence of this middle-sized flying-fox, although a small relative remains common. Just why it became extinct so early remains unclear, although hunting seems to have been one of the few human-caused factors that could have affected it. Its extinction may well have been detrimental to the entire island eco-system, for flying-foxes are important pollinators and dispersers of fruit that help maintain forest diversity.

1875
Broad-faced Potoroo
(*Potorous platyops*)

Last Record: about 1875. Distribution:
South-western Australia.

The tiny broad-faced potoroo is one of the most diminuitive and enigmatic of marsupials. It survived for just thirty-six years after the establishment of Western Australia's Swan River colony, where the city of Perth now stands, and almost nothing is known of its biology. The collector John Gilbert, who was working for John Gould, recorded all of our first-hand knowledge of the species in a sentence: 'All I could glean of its habits was that it was killed in a thicket surrounding one of the salt lagoons in the interior.' It seems to have inhabited a scrubby belt of vegetation between the forests of the south-west and the arid interior.

Only twelve specimens were ever collected, and of these only six came with records stating in what region they were caught. The Australian Museum in Sydney holds five specimens, and forty years after the creature was last heard of it lost a great opportunity to understand more about the species' biology. It was the only museum in the world to hold any complete bodies in spirit, but in 1913 the decision was made to skin the two spirit specimens it had held since the 1860s, to make study skins. The bodies, with all of their potential to tell us about diet, parasites, organ adaptations and DNA were simply thrown out.

The broad-faced potoroo vanished long before foxes or land clearing became widespread in Western Australia. It seems likely that either the cessation of Aboriginal burning or the arrival of cats caused its extinction.

1875

Newton's Parakeet

(*Psittacula exsul*)

Last Record: 14 August 1875. Distribution: Rodrigues, Mascarene Islands.

Newton's parakeet was restricted to a single island, Rodrigues, where it was once common. It was first described by a small band of Huguenots who settled on Rodrigues in 1691. They were the first humans ever to live on the island, and in many ways it was a paradise, for almost all of the animals they encountered were tame, the climate was benevolent and the soil fertile. The only hitch was that the group consisted of eleven men and no women. After two years they became desperate for female company and deserted the island in a brave attempt to reach Mauritius.

Francois Leguat, who documented the Huguenots' stay, wrote that, despite its small size, Newton's parakeet was very good eating. The men seem to have enjoyed large numbers of them, which they harvested easily by knocking them down with a stick. One bird, which was saved from the pot, learned to parrot both Flemish and French phrases, and the Huguenots took it with them when they left the island.

Only two specimens of Newton's parakeet survive in museum collections, each collected towards the end of the species' earthly tenure. It had become rare by the mid-nineteenth century and, perhaps too late, had also become very wary of humans. According to Leguat, the birds derived most of their nutrition from the nuts of a tree that produced an olive-like fruit.

1875

Labrador Duck

(*Camptorhynchus labradorius*)

Last Record: Autumn 1875. Distribution: North-eastern Coast of North America, from Labrador to New Jersey.

This striking duck undertook an annual migration, overwintering off the coasts of New Jersey and New England, then returning north to Labrador to breed in summer. For a species whose winter range included a well-populated region, remarkably little is known about it. This may be due to the fact that it was always apparently rather rare. John James Audubon's son (also named John) reported seeing a nest in Labrador that he believed belonged to this species, but much speculation remains concerning its breeding grounds. Writers suggest that islands in the Gulf of St Lawrence were a more likely site for it to lay its eggs. The only surviving eggs are held in a museum in Germany.

In winter it favoured southern sandy coasts, bays and inlets, where it searched for the shellfish that were its principal food. Fishermen occasionally record catching it on lines baited with mussels. Its beak was peculiarly soft and perhaps sensitive, and it may have probed in sediment for its food.

The Labrador duck was a wary bird that was difficult to shoot. Furthermore, its flesh was not good, and it often rotted before it could be sold. Just why such a species should vanish remains mysterious. Some authorities have suggested that changes in the molluscan fauna of the region were caused by human population increases, while others indicate that pillaging of its nesting sites was more likely. Whatever the case, the already rare duck slowly dwindled between 1850 and 1870, until the last authenticated specimen was shot off Long Island in the autumn of 1875, depriving the bird watchers of New England for all time of acquaintance with this mysterious creature. This final specimen now resides in the United States National Museum in Washington D.C., where it bears the number 77126. Only thirty-one museum specimens are known although more may be forthcoming, for recently a stuffed specimen turned up in a garage sale.

1876

Himalayan Quail

(*Ophrysia superciliosa*)

Last Record: 1876. Distribution: Foothills of the Western Himalayas, between 1340 and 1840 Metres Elevation.

The first Himalayan quail to come to the attention of Europeans was described in 1846. No one then knew precisely where it came from, although uncertain evidence pointed to an Indian origin. Then, between 1865 and 1868, several others were shot by hunters traversing the western Himalayas. There was a final sighting in the region in 1876.

Why such a small bird, inhabiting a remote region where humans have had such little impact, should become extinct, remains a riddle. Unless the species was already on the brink of vanishing it seems unlikely that the firepower of the British Raj was decisive. These quails were certainly not easy to hunt, keeping to areas of scrub on steep hillsides, and not flushing until almost trodden upon. They arrived in the western Himalayas in November, staying until June to feed upon grass seeds and insects. Where they spent the rest of the year is not known, but it seems possible that adverse changes in their breeding areas (which remain unidentified) proved fatal.

1876

Terror Skink

(Phoboscincus boucourti)

Last Record: before 1876. Distribution: New Caledonia.

The terror skink (following page) is known from just a single specimen, collected somewhere on the Pacific island of New Caledonia by a certain Monsieur Balanza before 1876. Its teeth are long, sharp and curved, indicating that it was a predator, which is unusual for a large skink, most of which are omnivorous. With the exception of a strange, land-going crocodile and a goanna that became extinct prehistorically, this skink, the largest reptilian predator on the island was about the same size as an Australian blue tongue lizard. Its diet is unknown, but it seems likely that it fed on larger invertebrates, other lizards and perhaps eggs and young birds. Herpetologists suggest that it might have been nocturnal.

A considerable amount of research has been done in New Caledonia in the years since the terror skink was last seen, but it has never been seen again. Recent investigation has, however, resulted in the discovery of a much smaller and often handsomely striped, living member of the same genus. Perhaps the introduction of cats, or the brown, black and Pacific rats that swarm in some parts of the island, drove its large relative into rapid extinction.

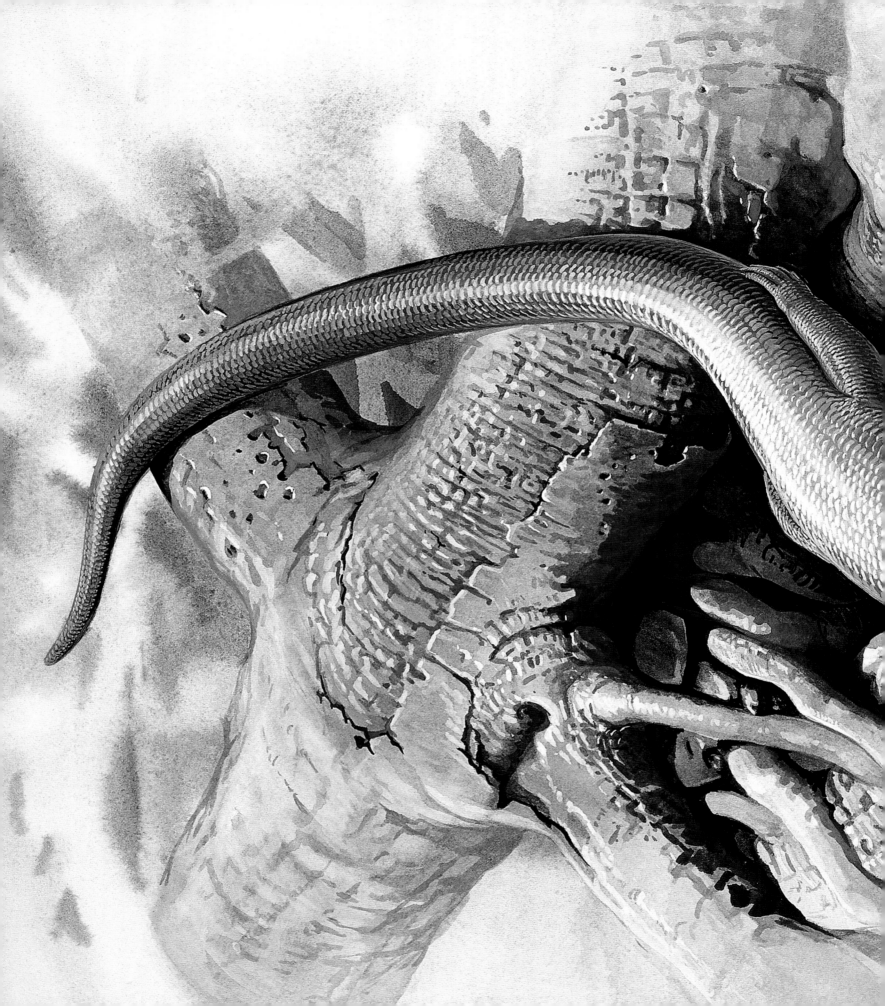

1876

Falkland Islands Dog

(Dusicyon australis)

Last Record: 1876. Distribution: West and East Falkland Islands.

The Falkland Islands dog was a canid whose ancestry is uncertain. Some scientists have argued that it is a relative of certain foxes that are found only in South America, while others have suggested that it is a kind of domestic dog, similar to the dingo, that was brought to the Falkland Islands by early Indian visitors. It was the only terrestrial mammal to inhabit the islands before European settlement, even adaptable island species such as rats and mice being absent. This fact supports the idea that it was carried to the Falklands by early Indian visitors, but others have dismissed this possibility, saying that no other evidence of such putative visits has been found.

Its diet consisted principally of birds, especially geese and penguins, and young seals, but it would also scavenge. It appears to have been readily tameable. A sea captain who visited the island in the eighteenth century took one to be his ship's pet. The experiment went well until the need arose to fire the vessel's cannon, at which the poor creature got such a fright that it leapt overboard and drowned. This familiarity with humans extended even to first meetings, with individuals wading out into the shallows to greet landing parties. It would often enter a camp searching for food, and was frequently killed by a hunter holding meat in one hand to entice it near, and a knife in the other. Such behaviour is common in long isolated island populations as well as in domesticated animals, so it does not help us in deciding the origin of the species.

Only eleven museum specimens are known, some consisting only of bones. The decline of the Falkland Islands dog began in 1839 when fur traders from the United States killed large numbers. In the 1860s Scottish settlers began raising sheep and an intensive poisoning campaign aimed at eradicating the creature was begun. It was very rare by 1870, and the last recorded individual was killed in 1876.

1877
Brace's Emerald
(*Chlorostilbon bracei*)

Last Record: 13 July 1877. Distribution: New Providence, Bahamas.

This brilliant jewel of a hummingbird is known from just a single male, collected by Lewis J. K. Brace 'about 3 miles from town, inland somewhat' on New Providence in July 1877. Its discovery was remarkable because the island had long supported a European population, and had been visited by several ornithologists, all of whom had somehow missed the species. This history led some ornithologists to suspect that the unique specimen was a vagrant that had been blown to the island from elsewhere. The trouble with this idea is that nothing quite like it had been found anywhere else.

In 1987 the mystery was solved. Palaeontologists working in caves on New Providence found the remains of three species of hummingbirds. One was from a large species known only from the fossils. A second was of a species still common on the island, while the third closely matched Brace's emerald.

The bones were testimony that Brace's emerald had lived on the island for many thousands of years. Somehow it had been reduced to an elusive, relict population by the late nineteenth century, and evidently eked out a living in the thick coppice surrounding the town of Nassau. Mr Brace arrived just in time to record the existence of this now vanished gem.

1884

Hawaiian Spotted Rail

(Pennula sandwichensis)

Last Record: about 1884. Distribution: Hawaii, Possibly Molokai, Hawaiian Islands.

The mysterious Hawaiian spotted rail was first recorded by European naturalists during Cook's third and fateful voyage between 1776 and 1780, when he discovered the remote island chain and was shortly after murdered by the Hawaiians. It must have been relatively common at that time, for it came to the attention of the Europeans, who soon discovered that it was suffi-ciently abundant to be served as a delicacy to the Hawaiian kings. Eighty years later, however, the bird known as *moho* to the Hawaiians had become exceedingly rare. The last specimen was collected in 1860, and the last sighting was made in 1884 or 1893.

Two colour forms have been recorded, a dark and a pale one, and it is still uncertain if one or two species of rail existed on the islands. It was an inhabitant of more open country, particularly the grassy areas below the level of the rainforest on the slopes of Kilauea, but also of scrub patches in forest. Its native name, *moho*, means 'the bird that crows in the grass'. It seems likely that the introduction of the black rat and cats—at or just after Cook's time—was a severe blow to the Hawaiian spotted rail, with perhaps the intro-duction of the mongoose in 1884 issuing the *coup de grâce*.

1889

Bonin Wood-pigeon

(*Columba versicolor*)

Last Record: 15 September 1889. Distribution: Peel and Nakondo-shima,
Ogasawara (Bonin) Islands, Japan.

The Bonin wood-pigeon is recorded from just two islands in the Ogasawara Group—Peel Island, where it was discovered by naturalists travelling with Captain Beechey on the *Blossom* in 1827, and Nakondo-shima, where the last specimen was taken in 1889. Friedrich von Kittlitz also collected it on Peel in 1828. The last animal seen was a male obtained by a Mr Holst, who was collecting for the British ornithologist Henry Seebohm. It was a large and beautiful pigeon, and may have always been rather uncommon.

Almost nothing is known of its natural history, although Errol Fuller, a researcher on obscure and extinct birds, considers that it fed on fruits, seeds and buds. Three specimens exist, in museums in Russia, Germany and Britain.

1889
Eastern Hare-wallaby
(*Lagorchestes leporides*)

*Last Record: Late 1889. Distribution:
South-eastern Inland Australia.*

This fleet and agile wallaby was once one of the most common of all marsupials on the inland plains of south-eastern Australia. Its habits were rather hare-like in that by day it sat still in a well-formed 'seat', usually in the shelter of a tussock. If approached too closely, however, it would bound off at great speed. John Gould recorded that one animal, which had been chased by his dogs for half a kilometre, 'suddenly doubled and came back upon me…I stood perfectly still and the animal had arrived within 20 feet before it observed me, when…instead of branching off to the right or left; it bounded clear over my head'. Another early naturalist reported that it could jump to a height of 1.8 metres, quite a feat for a hare-sized creature.

The last known specimen is a female collected by a Mr K. H. Bennett of Yandenbah, via Booligal, New South Wales. The Australian Museum had dispatched a supply of spirit and collecting materials by rail to Bennett on 23 August 1889 and the specimen was received at the museum by 4 January 1890. It was the only mammal forwarded to the museum by Bennett on this occasion, arriving with a number of birds collected in the Booligal area. It was purchased for five shillings, perhaps indicating that it was already rare.

Its final extinction is rather puzzling as it occurred before the onset of intensive agriculture throughout its distribution, and before the fox became abundant. Perhaps competition with cattle and sheep, which before 1890 were present in unsustainably high numbers, or changed burning patterns, or the spread of cats, proved to be decisive factors.

1891

Lesser Koa Finch

(Rhodacanthis flaviceps)

Last Record: October 1891. Distribution: Hawaii, Hawaiian Islands.

The lesser koa finch was collected on just a single occasion, by Lord Rothschild's collector Henry Palmer, in 1891. It was very similar to the greater koa finch, and was acquired at the same time as its near relative, both being found in koa trees where they had been feeding on seeds. Some ornithologists even consider these two species to be identical. These researchers argue that lesser koa finches were just juveniles of the greater species, although others argue that some of the lesser koa finches were adult.

Nothing further was recorded of the habits of this bird, whose discovery and evident extinction occurred on one and the same day.

1892

Ula-ai-hawane

(Ciridops anna)

Last Record: 20 February 1892. Distribution: Hawaii, Hawaiian Islands.

By the time this beautiful, diminutive bird was noticed by Europeans it was restricted to the largest island in the archipelago, Hawaii. In prehistoric times, however, it evidently had a much wider distribution, fossils of it having been found on Kauai, Molokai and Oahu. It is known from just five museum specimens, the first being collected by J. Mills, a shopkeeper on the island of Hawaii, around 1859. In Hawaiian its name means 'the red bird that feeds upon the hawane (*Pritchardia*) palm'. It was, according to those who knew it, wild, shy and pugnacious, never straying far from the palm that provided its food. It is thought to have fed on blossoms and unripe fruit.

Interest in the bird had grown to such an extent that by the 1890s rewards were being issued for specimens. They produced just a single result, a specimen brought to naturalist and collector George Munro, from near the headwaters of the Awini River on Mt Kohala in 1892. Forty-five years later, in 1937, Munro thought he saw the bird again, on the Kahua ditch trail, but he could not be sure. Hunting by Polynesians, and forest destruction to make gardens may have caused its initial reduction, although the spread of avian malaria and continued hunting seem to be the most likely causes of its final decline.

1892

Santa Cruz Tube-nosed Fruit-bat

(Nyctimene sanctacrucis)

Last Record: before July 1892. Distribution: Santa Cruz Group, Solomon Islands.

This bat, with its strange tube-nostrils, is known from a single specimen (a female) which was donated to the Australian Museum, Sydney, in 1892. It belongs to a genus of fruit-eating bats that has its distribution centred on New Guinea. The precise number of species of tube-nosed bats is still unclear, as some populations seem to grade into others. Nevertheless, up to four species can co-exist in certain parts of New Guinea. The single known specimen is one of the largest tube-nosed bats on record with a wingspan of around forty centimetres.

The Santa Cruz group of islands—which are the southernmost of the Solomon Islands—marks the easternmost limit of the genus' distribution. The largest island in the group is Ndende. Despite several expeditions there, including those equipped to detect such bats in the 1980s, the Santa Cruz tube-nosed fruit-bat has never been seen since. Many members of its genus prefer primary forest, and it seems possible that forest destruction caused its downfall.

1894
Red Gazelle
(*Gazella rufina*)

Last Record: before 1894. Distribution: Northern Algeria, Africa.

The gazelles are abundant and widespread creatures, occurring from Africa to China. There are sixteen species, only one of which has become extinct in recent times. The classification of some gazelles is still being determined, and a second form called *Gazella arabica*, which is of uncertain taxonomic status, is also known only from century-old specimens.

The red gazelle is identified from just three specimens, which were purchased in markets in Algiers and Oran, northern Algeria, during the late nineteenth century. They are held in museums in Paris and London, the last specimen being collected a few years before 1894 by E. Loder in Algiers.

As the living animal was never observed by a naturalist, nothing is known of its habits or ecology. It is thought, on the basis of the rich colouration of its coat, that it did not inhabit desert areas. Its distribution must have been limited, perhaps to the better watered mountain areas of North Africa, for it to succumb at such an early date.

1894

Kona Grosbeak

(Chloridops kona)

Last Record: 1894. Distribution: Hawaii, Hawaiian Islands.

The Kona grosbeak is one of the most mysterious of Hawaiian birds. It was known to Europeans for just seven years, and so elusive was it that it is one of the few species for which the native Hawaiians did not have a name. By the time it was discovered by Scott Wilson in 1887, it inhabited just ten square kilometres of lava flow and scrub on the slopes of Mauna Loa.

It was, according to one of the few Europeans who saw it, 'a dull, sluggish, solitary bird, and very silent— its whole existence may be summed up in the words "to eat". Its food consists of the seeds of the aaka [naio]…its beak is nearly always very dirty, with a brown substance adherent to it, which must be derived from the sandal-nuts.' The bird also ate caterpillars and leaves, and could often be located via the sound it made when cracking the kernels of its favourite food tree.

It is difficult to know why the species had such a restricted distribution when first discovered. It seems that it was more widespread in prehistoric times, and perhaps fossils of this obscure species will eventually be found elsewhere in the islands. Predation by the Pacific rat may have limited its distribution in Polynesian times, while avian malaria may have seen off the last few birds from their final, lava-girt refuge.

1894

Stephens Island Wren

(Xenicus lyalli)

Last Record: 1894. Distribution: Prehistorically, North and South Islands, New Zealand; Historically, Stephens Island, New Zealand.

Very few species have been exterminated by a single individual of another species, but such seems to have been the fate of this wren. Its last redoubt was Stephens Island in Cook Strait, between North and South Islands, where it survived until the New Zealand government built a lighthouse there in 1894. The lonely lighthouse-keeper, David Lyall, decided that he must have a cat, and over a year or so that solitary feline exterminated the entire species. It brought them, one by one, to the lighthouse-keeper's door and, thinking them strange birds, Lyall sent seventeen little bodies for identification to a museum.

This, however, is not the entire story of this curious little wren, the only known perching bird ever to lose the power of flight. Fossils reveal that before the arrival of the Pacific rat or kiore (*Rattus exulans*) in New Zealand around 1000 years ago Stephens Island wren was common throughout the archipelago. Predation by the rat eliminated it from over 99 per cent of its habitat before the arrival of Europeans. A single cat was then enough to push this precariously balanced species into oblivion.

Lyall was the only European ever to see the birds alive, and even he observed them just twice. He reported that they ran about like mice among the rocks of their island home. Twelve of Lyall's specimens are still held in museum collections.

1896

Greater Koa Finch

(Rhodacanthis palmeri)

Last Record: about 1896. Distribution: Hawaii, Hawaiian Islands.

Lord Walter Rothschild amassed an incomparable ornithological collection, and it is to him, or rather to his collectors, that we owe much of what we know about Hawaii's extinct birds. One such collector was Henry Palmer, who spent fifteen months collecting rarities in the Hawaiian Islands in the early 1890s, and to him fell the distinction of discovering several species that would vanish within a few decades. Given the large number of specimens sometimes shot by naturalists like Palmer, one wonders whether their knowledge was only gained at a cost of pushing already rare species closer to, or even over, the brink of extinction.

The greater koa finch was one of the largest members of the Hawaiian honeycreeper family to survive into modern times. It inhabited mountain forests between about 1000 and 1300 metres elevation, where it fed upon the seeds of the great koa (acacia) tree, and upon the caterpillars that infested it. The birds rarely descended from their lofty perch atop the koa, but if a hunter imitated their distinctive song they would readily approach within gunshot. The very last adult birds to be seen were busy collecting nesting materials and feeding well-grown young, when they were shot by a collector.

1896

Short-tailed Hopping-mouse

(*Notomys amplus*)

Last Record: June 1896. Distribution: Central Australia.

Some species of Australian mammals became extinct so rapidly after European settlement of the continent that the living animal was never described. Instead, they are known from a few bones. The short-tailed hopping-mouse, came perilously close to suffering this fate, for although its bones have turned up in deposits across a wide region of Australia, only two whole specimens were collected. These were secured by Patrick Byrne, the postmaster of Charlotte Waters, near Alice Springs, who probably obtained them from Aborigines visiting the outpost. Despite their large size for hopping-mice (they weighed perhaps eighty grams) they were not recognised as representing a distinctive species until several decades later. By then it was too late to go back and seek more information about them, for the species was already extinct.

The area around Charlotte Waters consists mainly of open gibber (stony) plains with desert grasses and low shrubs. There are also sand ridges in the area and the short-tailed hopping-mouse may have occupied either sand-ridge or gibber country, although the distribution of subfossil remains indicates that gibber plains were the more likely habitat.

1897
Nelson's Rice-rat
(Oryzomys nelsoni)

Last Record: 18 May 1897.
Distribution: Maria Madre Island,
Tres Marias Group, Mexico.

There were once around forty species of rice-rat. Many survive today, but several island forms, from the Caribbean to the Galapagos Islands, became extinct in early colonial times before a specimen was ever obtained or described by a naturalist.

Nelson's rice-rat inhabited damp thickets in the vicinity of springs near the summit of Maria Madre Island in the Tres Marias Group, off the coast of western Mexico. Four specimens were collected on 18 May 1897, by E.W. Nelson and E. A. Goldman. These are the only ones known. The introduction of rats and cats to its island home is thought to have caused its disappearance.

1898

Mamo

(Drepanis pacifica)

Last Record: July 1898. Distribution: Hawaii, Hawaiian Islands.

Although restricted to a single island, the mamo was once so common on Hawaii that the feathers of 80,000 individuals went into making a single cloak for the first King Kamehamea. The Hawaiians enforced strict conservation practices, such as plucking the prized yellow feathers from live birds before releasing them, and these may have contributed to its survival in the face of heavy hunting pressure until the 1880s.

Although the first mamos to reach European hands were collected by naturalists who accompanied Captain James Cook when he discovered the Hawaiian Islands on his third voyage, the species remains poorly known. Its call was a single, long and mournful note, and it seems to have moved about in small groups that were possibly families.

The last known mamo was shot by a Mr H. W. Henshaw, a collector for Lord Rothschild. He encountered a family of the birds in the woods above Kaumana. After stalking them patiently he shot at one while it perched atop a tall tree. He recalled:

> it was desperately wounded, and clung for a time to the branch, head downwards, when I saw the rich yellow rump most plainly. Finally, it fell six or eight feet, recovered itself, flew around the other side of the tree, where it was joined by a second bird, perhaps a parent or its mate, and in a moment was lost to view.

Hunting for plumes and specimens, and possibly the spread of avian malaria, seem to have been responsible for its extinction.

Chatham Islands Rail

(*Gallirallus modestus*)

Last Record: about 1900. Distribution: Prehistorically, Chatham Island; Historically,
Pitt and Mangere in the Chatham Islands.

The Chatham Islands are a remote group of temperate, forest-covered islands lying about 500 kilometres east of New Zealand. They are an ancient group that, until discovered by the Polynesians that made the archipelago home, had a rich fauna. One species that survived the onslaught was a flightless rail about the size of a blackbird. It resembled no other member of its genus, and ornithologists speculated that it represented a long-isolated, ancestral type.

It was highly secretive, being nocturnal and nesting in a hole in the ground. A single egg, about forty millimetres long and white with faint spotting, was collected, and represents all that is known about its nesting habits. After hatching, the chicks sought shelter in fallen hollow trees. Adults ate various invertebrates such as beetles and sandhoppers (amphipods).

The Chatham Islands rail survived on tiny Mangere Island long after having become extinct elsewhere in the group as a result of Polynesian and subsequent European settlement. Eventually Mangere Island itself was settled by Europeans and its vegetation grossly modified. Its forests were cut and burned and cats, goats and rabbits introduced. It is hard to determine what, among this catalogue of misfortunes, had the greatest impact on this modest rail. About twenty-six specimens made it into museum collections around the world between the time of its discovery in 1871 and its extinction, and it seems possible that hunting for museum specimens also hastened its decline.

1900

Chatham Islands Fernbird

(Bowdleria rufescens)

Last Record: about 1900. Distribution: Prehistorically, Chatham Islands;
Historically, Pitt and Mangere in the Chatham Islands.

The Chatham Islands fernbird was an obscure, reddish-brown bird about the size of a house sparrow. It was discovered in 1868 on Mangere Island by a Mr Charles Traill, who threw a stone at a small bird he saw in the undergrowth, killing it.

Nothing is known of the habits of the species, but its nearest relative, the fernbird of New Zealand, is a weak flier and inhabits dense vegetation around swamps and estuaries. Pairs are strongly territorial. The last museum specimen of the Chatham Islands fernbird was shot on Mangere Island by one of Lord Walter Rothschild's collectors around 1900.

1900

Guadalupe Caracara

(*Polyborus lutosus*)

Last Record: 1 December 1900. Distribution: Guadalupe Island, off Baja California.

The island of Guadalupe is a mere thirty-two kilometres long and just under ten kilometres wide. It lies 224 kilometres off the coast of California and is quite dry—ideal habitat for sheep and goats. The sheep-herders who settled there despised the caracara, perhaps blaming it for the increasingly hard times they faced before they abandoned the island in the dying years of the nineteenth century. Certainly they saw it as only a little less destructive than the devil himself. Collector Edward Palmer wrote that 'no bird could be a more persistent or cruel enemy of the poultry or domestic animals…seeming to delight in killing'.

At least one museum collector, however, seems not to have delighted in killing these birds. In 1887 W. E. Bryant visited the island. He saw just four individuals, one of which he shot and badly wounded. It was a male which:

> attempted to escape by running, with the assistance of his wings. Being over-taken and brought to bay, instead of throwing himself on his back in an attitude of defence, or uttering a cry for quarter, he raised his crest and with an air of defiance, calmly awaited death.

If only other shooters had seen dignity in such island-induced naivety, we might still have the caracara with us today.

The *calalie*, as it was known by the island's inhabitants, was indeed probably a nuisance to newborn lambs, but it was one that had an ultimate solution. Twenty-five years after Palmer wrote of the bird's cruel habits the Guadalupe caracara was no more. Like so many island birds, it showed little fear of man and none at all of firearms. It seems to have been most vulnerable when it came to drink, for then it would take no notice at all of the report of a rifle, and if a hunter missed he had all the time in the world to try again.

On 1 December 1900, collector Rollo Beck visited the now abandoned island. During his short visit he saw eleven of the birds fly overhead, and shot nine of them. He may have regretted his actions, for he wrote that he judged from the sighting and from the birds' tameness that they were abundant. It became obvious shortly thereafter that the species was in serious trouble. Indeed these were the last birds ever seen. Here, perhaps, is as clear a case as any of a species perishing at the hands of a bird lover.

1901

Greater Amakihi

(Hemignathus sagittirostris)

Last Record: 1901. Distribution: Hawaii, Hawaiian Islands.

The greater amakihi was so limited in distribution, and so obscure, that it apparently remained unknown even to native Hawaiians. It was found only in the dense, rain-drenched mountain forests in the Waikulu River Valley, where it was first discovered by Rothschild collector Henry Palmer in 1892.

The species was thereafter observed by R. Perkins in December 1895, who located a dozen birds, found singly or in pairs, by their distinctive call. During the twentieth century the thick woodlands that were its only home were felled to make way for sugar cane. Even if it had been able to adapt to other habitats, avian malaria or introduced predators would have been serious challenges.

1901
Pig-footed Bandicoot
(*Chaeropus ecaudatus*)

Last Record: 1901. Distribution: Inland Australia.

The pig-footed bandicoot (following page) was one of the very strangest of marsupials. The size of a kitten, it had long, slender limbs, the hind feet bearing a single, elongated toe like a tiny horse's hoof, while the forefeet bore two digits resembling miniature cloven hoofs. As its limbs suggest, it had a peculiar gait, being likened by a nineteenth-century naturalist to 'a broken-down hack in a canter, apparently dragging the hindquarters after it'.

Pig-footed bandicoots were never common, although the species was rather widespread. They appear to have been principally vegetarian, taking grass seeds in the wild, although in captivity they ate lettuce, bulbs and grasshoppers, and according to one observer they drank a good deal of water. By day they sheltered in a grass nest, from which they emerged in the evening to feed. Twins may have been normal, with breeding occurring between May and June.

Gerard Krefft, who collected eight specimens near the junction of the Murray and Darling rivers in 1857, took a drawing of a specimen with him to show to Aborigines, to help explain that this was the animal he was anxious to procure. Unfortunately, the only drawing he could obtain was of a specimen that had lost its tail, and his Aboriginal helpers brought him any number of common bandicoots with their tails screwed out, before arriving with two living pig-footed bandicoots. Krefft, who was on short rations at the time, studied them for some time before he was forced to kill them. He recorded that 'they are very good eating, and I am sorry to say that my appetite more than once overruled my love for science; but 24 hours upon "pig face" (*Mesembryanthemum*) will damp the ardour of any naturalist'.

The Australian nation came into existence through federation in 1901, the same year that the last pig-footed bandicoot specimen was secured. Interviews with Aborigines living in remote regions, however, suggest that the species survived long after this, finally becoming extinct in the western desert as late as the 1950s. Just which factors, such as the introduction of foxes, cattle, sheep, cats or changed fire regime was responsible for the extinction of this strange creature remains unclear.

PETER SCHOUTEN 99

Long-tailed Hopping-mouse

(Notomys longicaudatus)

Last Record: 1901.
Distribution: Inland Australia.

The rat-sized long-tailed hopping-mouse was one of the largest and most elegant of Australia's native hopping rodents. It was also very widespread in the drier regions of southern and central Australia and apparently favoured stiff, clayey soils for digging its burrows.

Almost nothing is known of its biology, for it became extinct before more than a handful of specimens had been gathered. John Gilbert recorded in 1843 that, despite its fondness for raisins, it was not as destructive to the stores of the settlers as smaller hopping-mice. A small fragment of skull found in 1977 in a recent owl pellet—a regurgitated bolus of fur and bones—near The Granites in the Northern Territory suggests that it may have survived longer than historical collection records indicate.

1902

Auckland Islands Merganser

(*Mergus australis*)

Last Record: 9 January 1902. Distribution: Prehistorically, throughout New Zealand and the Chatham Islands;
Historically, Campbell and Adams, Auckland Islands.

Mergansers are a predominantly marine group of ducks with long, thin, serrated bills. They are mostly fish-eaters and the centre of their distribution is in the northern hemisphere; only the Auckland Islands merganser and a Brazilian species are found south of the equator.

The Auckland Islands merganser was the smallest of all, weighing just under a kilogram. It also had the longest bill, and although its wings were reduced it could still fly.

It was eliminated throughout most of its range by Polynesians before European contact, surviving only on the inhospitable, subantarctic Auckland Islands south of New Zealand. This was probably marginal habitat, and may have supported just a few hundred birds. There it inhabited creeks, estuaries and sheltered bays where it preyed upon fish, shellfish and marine worms.

Although it could raise up to four young at a time, its tiny population size left it vulnerable to human exploitation. Pigs, rats and mice were introduced to the islands, and there were attempts at settlement, all of which must have had some impact. The final blow, however, probably came from museum collectors, who shot the remnants of the population during 1901–2. The last specimens to be seen were a pair, shot by a Mr Shattock on 9 January 1902.

1902

Piopio

(Turnagra capensis)

*Last Record: 1902. Distribution: Prehistorically, Stewart Island; Historically, North
and South Islands and Stephens Island, New Zealand.*

Recent studies suggest that the piopio was the most primitive member of the bower bird family, which is otherwise restricted to Australia and New Guinea. The two subspecies of piopio, as shown here, were very different. The North Island variant had a white throat and unstreaked underparts, while the South Island form had an olive throat and streaked underparts.

It inhabited forest and scrub from the coast to the mountains and took a wide variety of food, including berries, seeds and various invertebrates, often hopping about on the ground. At the commencement of European settlement it was widespread and, because of its trusting nature, was a familiar species. It was a common visitor to bush camps where it would take scraps of food. Its nest was built anywhere from a metre above the ground upwards and its clutch size was usually two.

The last known specimen was shot at Ohura, North Island, in 1902, but unconfirmed sightings continued until the 1960s. All nineteenth-century naturalists who considered its demise wrote that the brown, and possibly the black rat as well, were the main cause. Certainly the brown rat occurred in plague proportions on the west coast of the South Island between the 1880s and 1890s, during which time the local piopio population went into terminal decline.

1902

Martinique Giant Rice-rat

(*Megalomys desmarestii*)

Last Record: 1902. Distribution: Martinique, Caribbean.

The West Indies were once home to five species of giant rice-rats, all of which are now extinct. Three kinds survived into historical times, but only two of these are known from museum skins. About the size of a cat, the Martinique giant rice-rat was the largest of all. It was also the most abundant of the trio and the last to succumb.

It was recorded as being common on Martinique until towards the end of the nineteenth century, and was found in large numbers in coconut plantations, where it was considered to be a pest. It was also avidly

hunted for food, although its preparation was rather laborious, for in order to subdue its musky odour its hair was first singed off, then its body was exposed overnight and then boiled in two batches of water.

When pursued it often took to water, indicating a partially aquatic habit. Due to its propensity to damage crops, active attempts were made to exterminate it, but it remained common enough right through the 1800s to be a regular feature on the menus of restaurants on Martinique.

It may be one of the few species in this book whose extinction was not caused directly or indirectly by humans, but by a geological event. At 7.52 a.m. on 8 May 1902, Mt Pelee erupted with a ferocity that devastated the entire island. The town of St Pierre, a metropolis of 30,000, was engulfed by a swift superheated cloud of volcanic ejecta that vaporised much in its path. Those who arrived after the cloud passed were confronted with bizarre tableaux: wineglasses set on restaurant tables were melted into bizarre shapes, while the muscles of the café-goers were transformed to dried fibre. There was just a single human survivor—a condemned prisoner held in a dungeon deep underground. The island's unique rice-rat evidently perished either in this or subsequent eruptions during 1902, for it has not been heard of since.

Maclear's Rat

(*Rattus macleari*)

Last Record: 1903. Distribution: Christmas Island, Indian Ocean.

Christmas Island is a remote raised limestone atoll with a volcanic core lying some 300 kilometres south-west of Java in the Indian Ocean. At almost 14,000 hectares in extent, it was one of the very last, large tropical islands to be settled by humans. Although discovered in 1615 it remained unoccupied until 1886, when a fertiliser company was established there to mine phosphate. The island was home to two large and unique rats, one of which, Maclear's rat, was particularly abundant. An early resident wrote of it that:

> In every part I visited it occurred in swarms. During the day nothing is seen of it, but soon after sunset numbers may be seen running in all directions, and the whole forest is filled with its peculiar querulous squeaking and the noise of frequent fights ... As well may be imagined they are a great nuisance, entering the tents or shelters, running over the sleepers and upsetting everything in their search of food ... A number of dogs is kept to keep them in check, and near the settlement they are already certainly less numerous than elsewhere.

It was not dogs, however, that would bring about the downfall of this beautiful animal, but the accidental introduction of its near kin, the black rat, which arrived in the first years of the twentieth century. By 1902–3 the company doctor recorded seeing dead and dying Maclear's rats everywhere, even crawling about the island's paths in daylight. They had evidently been infected by a disease brought by their black cousins. A search in 1908 failed to find any Maclear's rats, although it is just possible that a few hybrids of it and the black rat survived the onslaught.

One curious consequence of the extinction may be the abundance of red land crabs that now inhabit the island, whose vast numbers and migration have become a major tourist attraction. They are barely mentioned by the first settlers, and it may be that, until its extinction, Maclear's rat kept their numbers in check.

1903

Bulldog Rat

(*Rattus nativitatis*)

Last Record: about 1903. Distribution: Christmas Island, Indian Ocean.

The higher hills and denser forests of Christmas Island once supported a most peculiar rodent. The bulldog rat had a short tail, and its back was covered in a layer of fat two centimetres thick. It lived in small colonies, in burrows among the roots of trees or under hollow logs in primary forest. It was a sluggish creature that never climbed and, according to an observer, when 'exposed to daylight, seems to be in a half-dazed condition'.

Almost nothing else is known of the habits of this unusual rat. It is certainly extinct, and we can only assume that it was carried off by the great murid epidemic that also destroyed Maclear's rat.

1904
Choiseul Crested-pigeon
(*Microgoura meeki*)

Last Record: January 1904. Distribution: Choiseul, Solomon Islands, Pacific Ocean.

The Solomons form a biologically rich and extensive island chain stretching east of New Guinea. Much of their fauna is found nowhere else, but some species are shared with New Guinea. The Choiseul crested-pigeon was unique to the Solomons and one of the largest and most spectacular birds found in the group. It was encountered by a European collector on just a single occasion, in January 1904, when Albert Meek, who collected natural history specimens for Lord Walter Rothschild, visited Choiseul Island in the eastern Solomons. The island was then a dangerous place, for its inhabitants were known to attack visitors without warning. Meek kept a boat on stand-by as he ventured into the swampy lowlands around Choiseul Bay, just in case the locals made an appearance. He emerged from the bush unscathed, and with six magnificent chicken-sized pigeons in hand, along with a single egg.

Members of the Whitney South Seas Expedition visited Choiseul in 1927 and 1929, and although they met natives who knew the species, they found no unequivocal evidence of its continued existence. The bird, older hunters recalled, roosted near to the ground in pairs or small groups, and also nested on the ground. They imitated its call with a low, trilling sound, and said it was called *kukuru-ni-lua*, meaning 'ground pigeon'.

The Whitney South Seas Expedition was, incidentally, one of the most famous ornithological expeditions of all time. It was funded by philanthropist Harry Payne Whitney, and operated through the American Museum of Natural History. For almost two decades, commencing in 1920, expeditioners systematically explored the islands of Micronesia, Polynesia and Melanesia for birds. They operated out of the seventy-five-ton schooner *France*, and made many remarkable discoveries, including that of the little shearwater, which had not been seen since 1769.

Although reports of Choiseul crested-pigeons were received from various parts of the Solomons as late as World War II, the species has now not been heard of for many decades. Hunters recalled how easy it was to take from its roost, and how cats, which were introduced to Choiseul in the early twentieth century, killed many. It seems likely that the introduction of cats—which reached other islands in the Solomons earlier—was in fact the principal cause of the bird's decline. It appears to have been an inhabitant of the lowlands and swamps, and doubtless ate fruit as do its surviving relatives, the goura pigeons of New Guinea.

PETER SCHOUTEN 98

1904

Molokai 'O'o

(*Moho bishopi*)

Last Record: 1904. Distribution: Molokai and Possibly Maui, Hawaiian Islands.

The Molokai 'o'o was known to Europeans for just twenty years. The species was described by Lord Walter Rothschild from specimens collected by Henry Palmer in 1892. It evidently kept to the treetops, where it fed on insects and nectar.

The last certain sighting was made by George Munro, who observed a group in 1904. Unsubstantiated reports were made from 1915 onwards, with one from as late as 1981, but the species is certainly extinct today. The cause of its extinction is unclear, but an ornithologist who reached the highest peak on Molokai in 1949 saw black rats climbing in the trees, where they represented a great danger to the naive island avifauna.

1907

Black Mamo

(Drepanis funerea)

Last Record: June 1907. Distribution: Molokai, Hawaiian Islands.

In June 1907 a collector named Alanson Bryan killed three birds he found flitting about in the undergrowth high in the mountains of Molokai. After shooting them he wrote, 'To my joy I found the mangled remains hanging in the tree in a thick bunch of leaves, six feet or more beyond where it had been sitting.' This was the last time anyone saw a living black mamo.

The species had been discovered just fourteen years earlier in June 1893, living high up in the mountains of Molokai, where it haunted the dense, mossy scrub in search of nectar. The birds nested in the underbrush, where the ground was boggy and soft. They were extraordinarily tame, and never flew far from the ground, spending their time in the understorey. Their discoverer, R. C. Perkins, observed them to 'sit quietly preening their feathers, when they have a very comical appearance, much stretching of the neck being necessary to enable them to reach the fore parts of the body with the tips of their long beaks'. Nectar formed a large part of their diet, and because of the mamo's large size they were able to dominate other, smaller competitors for flowers. Indeed individuals were often seen with their heads covered in pollen, presumably from the lobelia and ohia-lehua flowers that abounded in their habitat.

1907

Huia

(*Heteralocha acutirostris*)

Last Record: 28 December 1907. Distribution: North Island, New Zealand.

The huia was the largest and most peculiar member of a family of perching birds unique to New Zealand, characterised by fleshy wattles at the base of the beak. The huia was celebrated because the beaks of males and females were more different in shape from each other than in any other bird; the male had a stout, straight beak and the female a slender, curved one. So different are they that the sexes were initially described as belonging to different species. This peculiarity astonished nineteenth-century naturalists and there was considerable demand for specimens. As a result, hundreds of stuffed huia exist in the museums of the world.

The crow-sized huia was an inhabitant of dense forests, and habitually walked through the canopy or forest floor, being a weak flier. Its name is said to derive from its alarm call, which was a shrill whistle. The female laid between two and four greyish eggs with brown and purple markings in early summer.

The birds foraged in pairs and may have co-operated in obtaining food, which consisted of insects found in decaying wood, spiders and berries. The males would chisel out insects from wood much like a woodpecker, while the females would probe deep cracks and crevices.

By the time of European settlement the huia was already in decline and was restricted to the southern parts of the North Island. Matters worsened dramatically in 1902 when the Duke of York (later King George V) visited Rotorua and was given a huia tail-feather that he placed in his hatband. The price of feathers rose to a pound apiece as New Zealanders imitated their monarch. Despite regulations totally protecting the bird, which had been in place since February 1892, an illicit trade in feathers flourished.

A number of factors may have hastened the huia's end. Its tameness and the high demand for its feathers were doubtless important, but disease may also have played a role. Ticks found on specimens in museum collections belong to several Indian species which may have been carried on introduced birds, and which in turn may have brought disease to the population.

The last living huia were observed in a patch of forest just outside Wellington, where W. W. Smith saw three birds on 28 December 1907. Claims of other sightings were made well into the 1920s, and even more recent claims have been made, but all remain unsubstantiated.

1909

Bogota Sunangel

(Heliangelus zusii)

Last Record: 1909. Distribution: around Bogota, Colombia, South America.

The Bogota sunangel is known from a single specimen, which was purchased by Brother Nicéforo María, presumably at a market in Bogota, in 1909. Its status as a distinct species remained unrecognised until 1993, when a paper naming it was published. The specimen now lies in a drawer in a cabinet full of other extinct and endangered bird specimens in the Academy of Natural Sciences collection in Philadelphia. This cabinet, with all of its lifeless, feathered gems, is the only place that you can see some species today.

Nothing is known of the biology of this glorious hummingbird. It seems likely, however, that it inhabited a limited area of cloud forest near Bogota, which has since been cleared for the cultivation of coffee, maize or other crops. Many other inhabitants of such limited rainforest habitats may have accompanied it into extinction before we were even aware of their existence.

1910

Slender-billed Grackle

(Quiscalus palustris)

Last Record: about 1910. Distribution: Marshes around Upper Rio Lerma, Mexico.

The slender-billed grackle was a close relative of the common and widespread great-tailed grackle. It differed from its near relative in having an extremely limited distribution centred upon marshes around the upper Rio Lerma in Mexico, and in the distinctive plumage of juveniles. In many other ways, however, the two species appear to have been rather similar.

It is likely that the slender-billed grackle was exterminated by habitat alteration. Almost nothing was recorded of its biology before its extinction, and even its taxonomic status is currently in doubt, some researchers believing it to be a mere subspecies or variant of its great-tailed relative.

1911

Grand Cayman Thrush

(*Turdus ravidus*)

Last Record: 1911. Distribution: Grand Cayman, West Indies.

The Grand Cayman thrush was first described in 1886 and the last recorded specimen was obtained in 1911. It was rather similar to some mainland species and was an inhabitant of deep forest. By the early 1940s, when the final unconfirmed sighting occurred, no such forest remained on the island. All that seems to have been recorded of its natural history is that its song was a subdued warble. As was the case for so many now extinct island birds, the last confirmed sighting was fatal for the entire species, since the individual was shot by a professional bird collector. Even without such a *coup de grâce*, the species was almost certainly doomed by logging of the island's forest.

1911

Guadalupe Storm-petrel

(*Oceanodroma macrodactyla*)

Last Record: 1911. Distribution: Guadalupe Island, off Baja California.

The Guadalupe storm-petrel was a small seabird that nested only on the upper slopes of the higher peaks of Guadalupe Island. It arrived there around March each year, excavating burrows in the soft soil under pines and oaks, at elevations of 760 metres and above. There the birds laid a single whitish egg that was ornamented with minute lavender or reddish-brown spots. By the end of May they had raised their chicks, and dispersed once again into the endless expanse of the Pacific Ocean, though just where they went is a mystery.

Goats were introduced to Guadalupe by around 1850, and their disturbance of the mountain summits was severe. Worse was to come, however, for soon after this cats were introduced. These killers combed the nesting areas of the slight and defenceless birds, and ornithologists who visited the island early in the twentieth century reported finding the nesting grounds littered with the tiny, mangled bodies of storm petrels, the cats having killed more than they could eat.

'Here's a letter, here's a letter, for you, for you,' was how a visitor to the colony described the cries of the parent birds as they came to land to feed their young. The writing in that letter (if we allow the bird's DNA and behaviours to be viewed as such) had been shaped by a million or more years of evolutionary struggle while these tiny creatures battled for life on land and in the vastness of the sea. What lessons we might have learned from its text we shall never know, for we tore up the missive almost at the moment we became aware of it.

1914

Laughing Owl

(Sceloglaux albifacies)

Last Record: July 1914. Distribution: Prehistorically, Possibly Chatham Islands;
Historically, North, South and Stewart Islands, New Zealand.

The laughing owl was a medium-sized, long-legged owl that weighed just over half a kilogram. It seems to have preferred forest edges and rocky country, and may have fed primarily on lizards, earthworms, rodents, small birds and insects that it captured on the ground. Its nest was usually made in crevices among rocks.

Its common name comes from its call, said to have consisted of 'a loud cry, made up of a series of dismal shrieks frequently repeated'. Despite its unmusical vocalisations, it evidently had quite a good ear, for according to the eminent New Zealand ornithologist Sir Walter Buller:

> It could always be brought from its lurking place in the rocks, after dusk, by the strains of an accordion…the bird would silently flit over the face of the performer, and finally take up its station in the vicinity, and remain within easy hearing till [the music] had ceased.

By the time of European settlement it was already rare on the North Island, but it remained relatively common on the South Island until the 1880s. Captive specimens were kept in Britain in the 1870s, but there appears to have been no concerted attempt to breed them. Their temperament would have made them ideal pets. 'More gentle animals there could not be,' G. D. Rowley remarked, 'they allow themselves to be handled without any resentment.'

Unlike many of New Zealand's extinct birds, the last laughing owl was not shot by a collector, but was found dead in July 1914 at Blue Cliffs, South Canterbury. The introduction of rats, cats, stoats and weasels probably caused the extinction of this gentlest of owls.

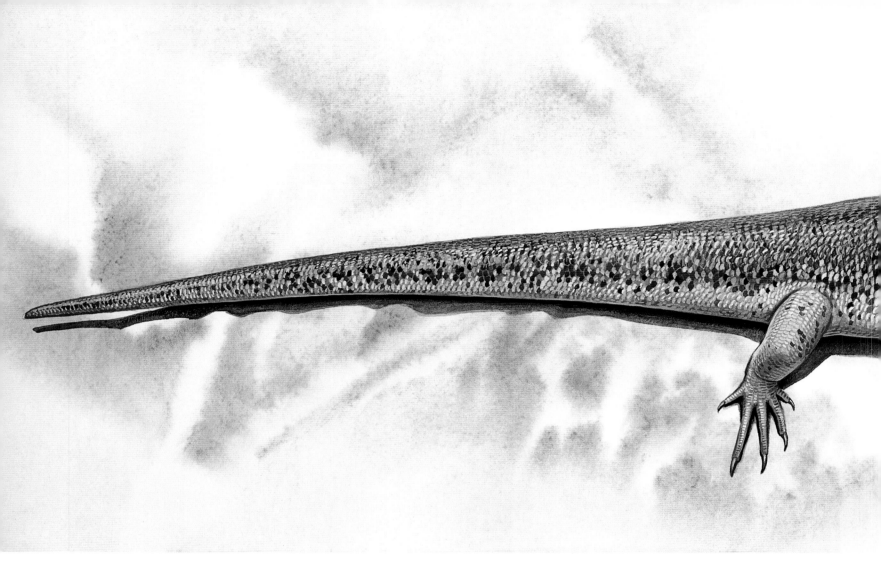

1914

Lagarto

(*Macroscincus coctei*)

Last Record: 1914. Distribution: Branco and Razo, Cape Verde Islands.

The Cape Verde Islands form an arid, rocky archipelago in the Atlantic Ocean off the coast of northwestern Africa. Rain falls on the islands between August and December, but for the rest of the year vegetation withers, making the area hostile for most forms of life. Despite their forbidding climate the Cape Verdes were once home to one of the world's most unusual lizards, the lagarto. When first noticed by Europeans it was restricted to two islands, Branco and Razo, both essentially bare rocks rising from the sea, though in earlier times it may have been more widespread.

If a stuffed specimen in the Muséum National d'Histoire Naturelle in Paris was not unduly stretched by the taxidermist who filled it with cotton wool, the lagarto was the largest skink ever to have lived, for the length of the head and body together is thirty-eight centimetres. It was covered in scales that seem to be

too small for such a huge skink, and its tail was prehensile, which seems superfluous given that no trees grew on its island home. Its strangest feature, however, were its teeth, which resemble those of an iguana, indicating that lagartos consumed much plant matter. They almost certainly supplemented their diet with the eggs and young of seabirds, for they were a major resource for part of the year. Indeed, given the barrenness of its island home, the lagarto ate almost anything else it could get its jaws around. It may have been nocturnal and, unlike some other skinks that give birth to well-developed young, it laid eggs.

Tradition among the Cape Verde Islands has it that the lagarto was once found on other islands in the group, but that it was hunted to extinction there during famines, surviving only on largely inaccessible Branco. A group of convicts banished to the rock in 1833 ate a large number of the lizard, but somehow it survived their depredations, turning up again in the 1870s after forty years of obscurity. It was, according to collectors, an easy species to catch.

When it was rediscovered some individuals were taken to Europe and kept in zoos. There one was photographed, giving us a clear idea of what it looked like. The last lagarto captured by a collector was taken by a German in 1914. The species may have survived a little longer, however, for the Cape Verde Islanders reported occasionally seeing them until the 1940s.

1914

Passenger Pigeon

(*Ectopistes migratorius*)

Last Record: 1 p.m., 1 September 1914. Distribution: Eastern North America.

The passenger pigeon (previous page) is renowned as being the most abundant bird ever to have existed. Its vast flights became legendary. Observers reported that they blacked out the sun as they passed, and that their droppings fell like snow. Their nesting aggregations were immense— some spanned over 160 kilometres, and so dense were the nesting pairs that their weight broke the stout limbs of trees. In all, some biologists calculate, passenger pigeons made up four North American birds out of every ten before their decline in the face of the European invasion.

Passenger pigeons were sleek, swift birds, capable of flying at speeds of nearly 100 kilometres per hour. John Audubon said of them that 'when an individual is seen gliding through the woods and close to the observer, it passes like a thought, and on trying to see it again, the eye searches in vain; the bird is gone'. The birds seem to have lived life at a hectic pace. The massive flocks wheeled as they fed like a giant threshing machine. They would eat acorns, nuts, caterpillars and much else that came their way, and if they found a more delectable morsel they would eject from their crop whatever they had in it to make room for the tastier morsel. Their single egg hatched after twelve or thirteen days, and the squab was fed by the parents for just two weeks. The adults then left the young on its own. The chicks scrambled to the ground, fending for themselves as best they could, and if they survived were flying and feeding independently only thirty days after the egg had been laid. Somehow the young would then join the great aggregations, and reproduction would start over again.

The bounty they presented must have seemed limitless to the pioneers, and hunters killed without thought for the morrow. Indeed, in one hunting competition, the winner had to tally 30,000 birds before the trophy was his. The killing was having an impact, however, and by the 1870s the flocks were on the wane. Once reduced, their nestings seem to have been less successful, and in just a few decades the birds had become exceedingly rare. The last wild living bird to be shot was killed in Ohio in 1900, while the last passenger pigeon on earth died in Cincinnati Zoo in the early afternoon of the first day of September 1914. It was, ornithologist Errol Fuller claims, perhaps the only species whose passing is known with such precision.

1918
Carolina Parakeet
(Conuropsis carolinensis)

Last Record: February 1918. Distribution: Eastern North America.

The vast majority of parrots are inhabitants of the southern hemisphere, and in this the Carolina parakeet (following page) was an anomaly, for its habitat once stretched to New York and the Great Lakes. Even in mid-winter it would venture as far north as Albany, its colourful flocks making a wondrous contrast with the leafless trees and snow-covered ground.

Records show that the Carolina parakeet suffered wherever it contacted the expanding wave of European settlement. The felling of the forests doubtless affected it, but hunting was also a powerful factor in its decline, for it was ruthlessly hunted as a pest, and its sociability made it particularly vulnerable to a man with a gun. Its native food consisted of seeds of various plants, with the cockleburr being a favourite. The coming of European agriculture provided an irresistible attraction, and orchards and fields were soon a major source of food.

Its flocks were once so vast that John Audubon commented that when plundering orchards they 'present to the eye the same effect as if a brilliant coloured carpet had been thrown over them'. Indeed, when Audubon came to illustrate the species, he chose his specimen from a basketful of birds destroyed by hunters 'at a few shots'. The reason that so many birds fell at one shot lay in their peculiar habits, for they would fly around a wounded or dead companion, squawking and screeching until they too fell to the hunter. This fateful habit may have developed in response to non-human predators, where it may have served both to frighten off the attacker and to familiarise the surviving birds with the danger it presented. Curiously, in other respects it was a wary bird.

The Carolina parakeet favoured areas near water, and where great, hollow stumps existed. They would crowd inside these to roost at night, doubtless for warmth, clinging to the wood with their beaks and claws. Nests were built in tree hollows, but there are also some records of flimsy nests being made on branches. In any case, their dependence on large, hollow trees left them vulnerable to European forestry practices.

They were still common enough in the 1880s that they were sold live by the dozen for just $2.50 per head, and it was in this way that Cincinnati Zoo received its last specimens. Included in the shipment was a bird the zookeepers dubbed Inca. He was destined to be the last recorded member of his species, and he survived in captivity until either 14 or 21 February 1918 (the records are unclear). After his death the body was lost, and despite several unconfirmed records from Okeechobee County in Florida in the 1920s and 1930s, no uncontested sightings have been made since. It was also in Florida that the last wild bird was taken, on 4 December 1913. Today North America is a poorer place for not having parakeets to enliven its winter. Around 700 skins of this lost species are housed in museums around the world.

Robust White-eye

(Zosterops strenuus)

Last Record: about 1918. Distribution: Lord Howe Island, Australia.

Until 1788 Lord Howe Island was the last truly virginal island in the south-west Pacific. Unlike the white gallinule, which seems to have vanished soon after people arrived there, the robust white-eye survived over a century of human contact and, until the time of World War I, was a familiar sight to the island's inhabitants.

Even a century ago it was known that rats could be highly destructive to island faunas, and, in an attempt to keep rodents from the island, vessels visiting Lord Howe were required by law to anchor offshore and ferry their cargo in lighters. The system worked well until the night of 18 June 1918, when the SS *Makambo* ran aground. Her captain had suffered a blackout while at the bridge, and the Burns Philp liner ran onto rocks. She was successfully refloated but the pumps could not cope and the stricken vessel was deliberately run ashore at Ned's Beach. Amid the chaos, no one noticed the rats swimming to the beach. They were black rats, and were the first murids ever to reach the island. It was a year before their presence started to be noticed, but thereafter their numbers built quickly. By 1921 visiting naturalist Allan McCulloch was lamenting that 'one can scarcely imagine a greater calamity in the bird world than this tragedy which has overtaken the avifauna of Lord Howe Island'.

The alarmed islanders introduced owls (which had not existed there before) to control the rats, but that only made matters worse as the owls preyed on the native island life as well. The rats, and to a lesser extent the owls, soon wrought a wave of destruction that was to carry away a whole suite of species—lizards, insects, land snails and of course birds, of which the robust white-eye was one.

The sparrow-sized white-eyes were known to the island's inhabitants as 'big grinnels' and before the arrival of the rats there were thousands of them. Indeed, they were disliked because they raided crops and sucked the eggs of other birds. The rats worked quickly, however, and just ten years after they first swam ashore no more big grinnels were to be seen. Today black rats still exist in large numbers in parts of the island.

Red-moustached Fruit-dove

(Ptilonopus mercierii)

Last Record: 1920s. Distribution: Nuku Hiva and Hiva Oa, Marquesas Islands, Pacific Ocean.

The Marquesas are a remote, scattered island group in the central Pacific. They were not a popular destination with the crews of whaling vessels, or any European voyagers, for the islanders earned a bad reputation after they attacked and took a number of vessels in the early days. This unpopularity evidently spared islands in the Marquesas group an invasion of rats. It did not, however, protect the whole Marquesan fauna from extinction, for one of the world's most beautiful fruit-doves was once an inhabitant of the archipelago, and it was to fall prey to mysterious forces by the early twentieth century.

The island of Nuku Hiva rises abruptly from the blue Pacific to over 1000 metres elevation. It is a rugged island and a natural fortress, you might think, for endangered species. Tragically this did not prove true for the beautiful red-moustached fruit-dove (following page), which was last recorded there in 1849. A distinct race of the bird inhabited Hiva Oa in the same island group, and it was still to be seen as late as the 1920s. Recent searches, however, have failed to find the Hiva Oa form of the red-moustached fruit-dove, and it too is now considered extinct.

1927

Paradise Parrot

(Psephotus pulcherrimus)

Last Record: November 1927. Distribution: North-eastern Australia.

The paradise parrot (previous page) once inhabited woodland and grassland over a broad swathe of Australia's north-east; from northern New South Wales to the Rockhampton area of Queensland. There this swift flier lived in pairs or small groups. Some early records indicate that it burrowed into steep riverbanks, hollowing out a chamber within which to lay its eggs; but more often it would burrow into termite mounds. There the birds would excavate a narrow tunnel that led to the brood chamber, within which three to five eggs would be laid directly upon the loose earth of the mound itself, no nesting material being utilised.

The species was becoming rarer towards the end of the nineteenth century, and by 1915 fears were held by some that it was already extinct. A search was begun by the ornithologist Alec Chisholm and in 1921 a single pair was located in the Burnett River region of Queensland. These two birds were sighted on occasion until 1927. Then one day they flew off from their observer, Mr C. H. H. Jerrard, and were seen no more. Only a handful of unsubstantiated sightings have been made since.

Jerrard described the song of the male as:

> very mixed and very animated…his whole body vibrated with the force and intensity of his musical effort, imparting an agitated motion to the long tail which bore adequate testimony to the vim of the performance. It all seemed to indicate a very intense little personality under the beautiful exterior.

Paradise parrots fed principally upon grass seeds, and were said to strip seeds from the standing stalks. The introduction of sheep and cattle into its habitat may well have drastically limited its food supply, particularly if it favoured the grass species eaten by livestock, but it seems that collecting for the pet trade must also bear some responsibility. Both factors, in conjunction with a drought in the 1920s, may have combined to eliminate the species.

Darwin's Rice-rat

(Nesoryzomys darwini)

Last Record: 16 January 1929. Distribution: Indefatigable Island, Galapagos Islands, Pacific Ocean.

The Galapagos are a dry, volcanic group of islands lying off Ecuador in the far eastern Pacific. They are famous for their unique and fearless fauna, and for the role they played in the formulation of Charles Darwin's theory of evolution by natural selection. Although better known for their birds and reptiles, the island group once also supported a diverse array of native rodents. Of the four species of rice-rats originally inhabiting the island group, just one still exists, and two are known only from bones. All were probably nocturnal rodents that inhabited burrows or rock crevices under bushes.

Darwin's rice-rat (following page) is known from just four specimens, all collected by Frank Wonder between 12 and 16 January 1929 at Academy and Conway bays on Indefatigable Island. Recent searches have yielded only introduced rats on Indefatigable. Competition with or disease brought by introduced black and brown rats appears to have caused the extinction of most of the Galapagos rice-rats, for the only surviving species inhabits rat-free Fernandina Island.

1931

Pemberton's Deer-mouse

(Peromyscus pembertoni)

Last Record: 26 December 1931. Distribution: San Pedro Nolasco Island, Gulf of California.

The deer-mice are a highly successful group, with more than fifty species distributed throughout North and Central America. Only two species are known to have become extinct in recent times. One, *P. nesodytes*, inhabited San Miguel Island off southern California. It became extinct as a result of human-induced change some time between 2000 years ago and 1860, and was never described or recorded as a living animal.

Pemberton's deer-mouse, which inhabited San Pedro Nolasco Island, survived until at least 1931. On 26 December of that year Dr Willian Hendy Burt of the California Institute of Technology visited the island and collected twelve specimens. The species, which was never seen thereafter, was named for R. J. Pemberton in recognition of his support in helping complete the survey of the islands in the Gulf of California that resulted in the sighting of this species before it slipped into oblivion.

Ryukyu Wood-pigeon

(*Columba jouyi*)

Last Record: 1930s. Distribution: Ryukyu and Borodino Islands, Japan.

This large, blackish pigeon was an inhabitant of heavy forest on a number of islands among the Ryukyu group in Japan's southern waters. At around forty-five centimetres long it was a large species, making it a desirable item for the pot.

Nothing is known of the habits of this handsome, subtly iridescent bird. Habitat destruction, particularly felling of the dense forests it frequented, hunting, and possibly the introduction of predators or disease, caused a rapid decline. Its island habitat continues to support a number of unique species that, unless they are protected, may soon follow the wood-pigeon into oblivion.

1933
Lesser Stick-nest Rat
(Leporillus apicalis)

Last Record: Afternoon, 18 July 1933. Distribution: Southern Inland Australia.

The presence of the lesser stick-nest rat was obvious to early explorers and biologists, for the large mounds of sticks it accumulated to construct its nests were a prominent part of the landscape, the largest being three metres long and a metre high.

It was, to judge from the records of Gerard Krefft, a member of the Blandowski Expedition to the junction of the Murray and Darling rivers in 1856–57, an easily tameable and delightful creature. He recorded that he had 'frequently taken eight to ten out of a hollow tree and tamed them so that they kept about the camp, mounting the supper table at tea time for their share of sugar and damper'. Krefft also had the unique opportunity, among white men at least, of turning the tables on the rat and having it for dinner, for he recorded that 'the flesh is white and of excellent flavour'.

The last known specimens were collected in the Musgrave Ranges in central Australia in 1933 by Norman Tindale, anthropologist at the South Australian Museum. The event was captured on film, a unique event in the annals of animal extinction. On 18 July 1933, Tindale, exploring west of Mt Crombie, wrote in his journal, 'Left camp at 2.30 pm. Saw several more of the mound building rats nests; the natives set fire to each of them & secured two rats. Secured a cinematographic film of the hunt.' The specimens are held in the South Australian Museum, their registration numbers being M4073 and M4074. They make a brief appearance in Tindale's film, held aloft in the hands of their Aboriginal captors, who had set the stick-nests alight and chased the occupants through the scrub.

It has been suggested that the cause of this rat's decline was competition with cattle and sheep, for it was a herbivore and may have been unable to compete with the introduced species. There is a faint hope that it survived until at least 1970. In that year an experienced bushman deposited some equipment in a cave west of the Canning Stock Route in the Western Australian outback. He covered it with a tarpaulin, and when he returned several weeks later he found a large, attractive rodent living under it. He caught it, examined it closely, then let it go. From his description, it is just possible that it was a lesser stick-nest rat.

1934
Hawaii 'O'o
(Moho nobilis)

Last Record: about 1934. Distribution: Hawaii, Hawaiian Islands.

As its Latin name suggests, this was the royal bird of Hawaii, and its feathers were a key decorative element in the robes and capes worn by the island's nobility. When discovered by Europeans in the late eighteenth century it was abundant and could be seen from the coastal areas up to the high forests. It frequented the treetops, and was wary. Its nest was never seen by a European naturalist and its eggs remain unknown. Its call was a double-syllable, reflected in its common name. Although primarily a nectar feeder, it would also consume fruit and insects.

It suffered a major decline during the nineteenth century, however, as late as 1898 hunters in the Wailuku area of Hawaii killed a thousand individuals of this now extinct bird. They had evidently discovered a hitherto overlooked population, for by that date it was considered rare.

By the early twentieth century the Hawaii 'o'o was in very serious trouble, and around 1934 its call was heard for the last time. It is possible that habitat disturbance affected it, for it required tall trees, but other factors were doubtless also at work. Avian malaria, which was introduced to the Hawaiian Islands by the early twentieth century, may have been the principal cause of its extinction.

1935
Desert Rat-kangaroo
(Caloprymnus campestris)

Last Record: 1935. Distribution: Central Australia.

The driest, hottest and most desolate environments in Australia were once home to the desert rat-kangaroo (following page). Around the size of a small rabbit, it was one of the most beautiful and graceful of marsupials. Most of the smaller desert creatures seek shelter in burrows or caves during the heat of the day, but the desert rat-kangaroo made do with a flimsy nest. At night it would emerge and feed where the forbidding gibber plains meet the loamy flats created by episodic flooding of the inland waterways to the north-east of Lake Eyre.

It was a solitary creature that was so independent of water it even shunned the succulent plants of the sandhills. Just how it survived in such an inhospitable region is a riddle. Indeed, the creature itself was an enigma for nearly a century. It was first recorded by Europeans around 1841 and was not considered rare at the time, but ninety years were to pass before a second sighting was made. That sighting was reported to Hedley Herbert Finlayson, honorary curator of mammals at the South Australian Museum, who spent parts of the next four years studying the creature. In a popular account of his adventures in central Australia, he recalled his first encounter with the tiny animal that the Aborigines knew as the *oolacunta*:

> The six of us rode east in the early morning, and on a sand-hill picked up fresh oolacunta tracks crossing to a flat on the far side. We followed them out till we lost them in the gibbers; then we rode out to a half-mile front and rode slowly south, each man scanning every lump and tussock for a possible nest. We had ridden less than half an hour when there came a shrill excited 'Yuchai' from the horse-boy furthest out, and the chase was on…Tommy came heading back down the line towards the sand-hill, but it was only after much straining of eyes that the oolacunta could be distinguished—a mere speck, thirty or forty yeard ahead. At that distance it seemed scarcely to touch the ground; it almost floated ahead in an eerie, effortless way…as it came up to us I galloped alongside to keep it under observation as long as possible. Its speed, for such an atom, was wonderful, and its endurance amazing.

> We had considerable difficulty heading it with fresh horses. When we finally got it…it had run us 12 miles; all under such adverse conditions of heat and rough going as to make it almost incredible that so small a frame should be capable of such immense output of energy… All examples…behaved similarly…They persisted to the very limit of their strength, and quite literally, they paused only to die.

In 1935 the last report of a sighting arrived at the museum from the far north of the state, and then the desert rat-kangaroo was seen no more. Although it is currently considered extinct, this peculiar history gives a faint hope that it may still survive somewhere in the vast interior of the Australian continent.

1936
Pink-headed Duck
(Rhodonessa caryophyllacea)

Last Record: about 1936. Distribution: Floodplains of the Ganges and Brahmaputra, India.

Bengal is today a great hive of human activity, but just over a century ago extensive swamps and marshes existed where cities and farms now lie; these marshes were the favoured haunt of the pink-headed duck. A relative of the pochards, its pink neck, head and (in the male) beak, gave it a striking appearance, and one which members of the Raj valued as a trophy.

Pink-headed ducks were apparently omnivorous, feeding on waterweed and invertebrates. They preferred the open waters of lagoons and ponds surrounded by dense vegetation. There they would gather in sixes and eights, and occasionally in flocks of up to forty. They bred in May, constructing their nests in dense grass, often far from the water's edge.

Although never common, the opening up of their habitat to development towards the end of the nineteenth century meant that they were regularly sold in the markets of Calcutta. By around 1900, however, they were rarely seen. The last sighting of a wild individual occurred in 1926, but a few lived on in captivity. Up to thirteen pairs were kept at Foxwarren Park, Surrey, in the late 1920s, where they thrived but did not breed. Gradually they died off, their demise unnoticed by the larger world. Just when the last survivor (rumoured to be a male) perished is unclear, some sources suggesting 1936, others holding out for death in old age as late as 1945.

Thylacine

(Thylacinus cynocephalus)

Last Record: Night of 7 September 1936. Distribution: Prehistorically, Australia and New Guinea; Historically, Tasmania.

The thylacine was the largest marsupial predator to have survived into historic times. Before the introduction of the dingo to mainland Australia around 4000 years ago it was widespread on the mainland and in New Guinea. When first encountered by Europeans in the early nineteenth century it was restricted to the island of Tasmania. There, however, it occurred in a variety of habitats, but not apparently the dense rainforests of the south-west.

Thylacines were rather wolf-like in shape, males reaching around thirty-five and females twenty-five kilograms in weight. They seem to have hunted singly, in pairs and in family groups (male, female and one to three young), pursuing wallabies and other prey by scent, eventually running them to exhaustion or into ambush.

Lairs were often located among rocks, and young stayed with the female until they were well grown and able to hunt independently. The Tasmanian Aborigines occasionally hunted them, but would build a curious shelter over the bones, believing that if they were rained upon then very bad weather would follow.

Thylacines were persecuted into extinction. A bounty was paid on scalps and, as they became rarer, live and even dead animals commanded ever higher prices. The species was finally protected by law in Tasmania in 1936, the year of its extinction. The law came far too late, for the last capture of a wild thylacine had occurred three years earlier.

The last thylacine to walk the earth was a female kept in Beaumaris Zoo near Hobart. Personnel problems developed at the zoo during 1935–36, which meant that the animals were neglected during the winter. The thylacine was 'left exposed both night and day in the open, wire-topped cage, with no access to its sheltered den'. September brought extreme and unseasonal weather to Hobart. Night-time temperatures dropped to below zero at the beginning of the month, while a little later they soared above 38 degrees celsius. On the night of 7 September the stress became too much for the last thylacine and, unattended by her keepers, she closed her eyes on the world for the last time.

It is possible that a few wild individuals roamed the island for a decade or two after this, for authentic-sounding reports were received until at least the 1940s. One concerned an old 'dogger' who claimed to have 'put up a slut and three cubs out of a patch of man-ferns' in the area that was shortly after flooded to form Lake King William. According to author Eric Guiler, who interviewed the hunter, he 'continually dodged the issue as to whether the thylacines were killed or not' after the man turned his dogs onto them, but Guiler strongly suspected that they were. Now all hope is lost, for many expensive searches have been made, yet no thylacine sighting has been authenticated for many years.

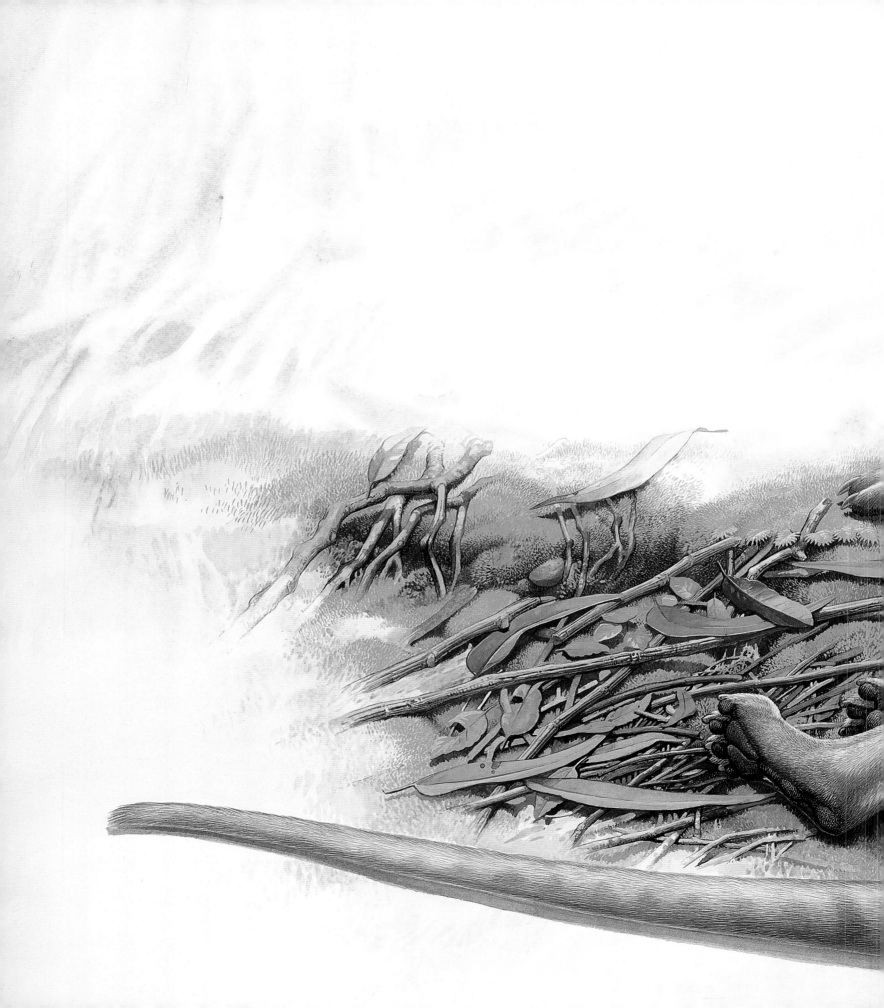

PETER SCHOUTEN '99

Toolache Wallaby

(Macropus greyi)

Last Record: 30 June 1939. Distribution: South-eastern South Australia and South-western Victoria, Australia.

The toolache—pronounced too-lait-shee—wallaby (previous page) was widely regarded by early observers to be the most elegant, graceful and swift member of the kangaroo family. It was common within a limited distribution, which unfortunately coincided with a region of fertile soils and reliable winter rainfall that was quickly taken up by settlers.

The fur of this curious wallaby was fine, and was frequently observed to have alternating bands of darker and lighter grey across the back. The bands differed not only in their colour but in the texture of the fur. This marking may have varied seasonally or between individuals. Its hopping was also unusual, for it characteristically took two short hops then a long one.

It was a gregarious species, and groups were loyal to a particular location. People interviewed during the 1920s remember that there was a patch of broom-brush near Clay Wells in South Australia from which toolaches could be reliably flushed provided that they had not already been disturbed that day. Their speed was legendary. Greyhounds could catch them if they got a close start, but most other dogs were left far behind. They never hurried until the dogs got close, and then bounded rapidly away. One individual was chased on horseback for six kilometres, and when it escaped through a fence its speed was still unabated.

The toolache was affected by hunting, mostly for the fur trade or for sport, and by pastoralism. Despite considerable pressure from these activities it remained relatively common until 1910. By 1923, however, it had become exceedingly rare, with the last known group of fourteen inhabiting Konetta sheep run near Robe on the South Australian coast. Professor Wood Jones of the University of Adelaide had become alarmed at the perilous state of the species and in May 1923 organised an attempt to capture some individuals of this last remnant for relocation to a sanctuary on Kangaroo Island. This attempt, along with another in 1924, failed. Just four individuals were captured, all dead or dying. The creatures had been driven too hard, and had died from exhaustion and shock.

The publicity given to this failed conservation effort encouraged local hunters to harass the last remnant to obtain a pelt or trophy. In 1927 a female was finally captured. She had a young in her pouch but it did not survive. Despite numerous efforts to find her a mate, no other toolache was ever taken alive. She lived in captivity at Robe for twelve years, finally succumbing in the winter of 1939.

Anecdotal reports of toolache sightings have continued to the present time. None have been substantiated, but one report, of the capture of an animal by two greyhounds owned by Albert Joseph, in 1943, has some credence.

Several factors were probably responsible for the decline of the species, including hunting, land clearance and the introduction of the fox. The final blow, however, was delivered through a bungled conservation attempt and subsequent trophy-hunting.

1943

Laysan Rail

(Porzana palmeri)

Last Record: 1943. Distribution: Laysan Island, Hawaiian Islands.

Laysan Island is a tiny, Pacific landmass just a few kilometres in extent. Once an island as grand as Hawaii itself, it played host to several unique species. The Laysan rail had no fear of man, even supping on the yolks of eggs that bird-hunters were blowing. Eggs were laid between April and July, the chicks resembling, according to one observer, 'a black velvet marble rolling along the ground. Its little feet and legs are so small and move so fast they can hardly be seen.' To survive it had to be resourceful; it scavenged flesh, ate seeds, and was agile enough to snatch flies from the air. Shortly after dark every rail would call out a short series of chattering, warbling notes, then all would be silent. One early ornithologist described the sound as being similar to 'a handful or two of marbles being thrown on a glass roof and then descending in a series of bounds'.

The bird's woes began in the early twentieth century; guinea pigs and rabbits were introduced to supply a meat cannery that never materialised. By the 1920s the rails were gone. The species survived, however, for in 1891 a few had been moved to Eastern Island. In 1913 others were taken to Lisianski Island, though rabbits followed, exterminating the rail there. Yet those on Eastern Island thrived, and birds were moved to nearby Sand Island to increase their number. In 1943, a US Navy landing craft drifted ashore, and the rats it carried invaded both Eastern and Sand islands; within two years the last populations were gone.

1945

Wake Island Rail

(Gallirallus wakensis)

Last Record: about 1945. Distribution: Wake Island, Pacific Ocean.

Wake Island is a remote speck of land lying approximately halfway between Japan and Hawaii. For thousands of years it provided a secure refuge for a curious rail, similar to, but smaller and darker than the related banded rail. It bred between July and August, and seems to have eaten just about anything that came its way, including molluscs, insects and worms. Its call was a low chattering sound or a gentle click.

All went well for this mild creature until the outbreak of hostilities between the US and Japan in 1941. Its island home then assumed enormous strategic importance, and was quickly occupied by invading Japanese forces. As the tide of war turned the Japanese soldiers faced starvation, and appear to have eaten every last rail on the island. By the time peace dawned over the Pacific in 1945 the world was a much impoverished place, for the Wake Island rail was gone, a victim of immense human upheaval.

1952

Caribbean Monk Seal

(Monachus tropicalis)

Last Record: 1952. Distribution: the West Indies; the Coasts of Florida,
Yucatan and Eastern Central America.

The three species of monk seals are true seals, belonging to the family Phocidae. They are unusual in having a tropical distribution, originally being found in the Hawaiian Islands, and the Mediterranean and Caribbean seas. Their common name results from a cowl of fatty skin on their necks, which reminded fishermen of the habits of the monks of old. They are the most ancient of seals and are, in a sense, living fossils.

Although the Caribbean monk seal (following page) was seen during Columbus' second voyage in 1494, and has been hunted almost continuously ever since, almost nothing was recorded of its biology or habits. It was large (up to 2.4 metres long) and was reputed to be very tame. The peak of pupping probably occurred in December.

Hunting for skins and oil had already made it scarce by the mid-nineteenth century, while during the twentieth century it was persecuted by fishermen who accused it of competing for fish. The last reliable record is of a small colony on Seranilla Bank, between Jamaica and Honduras, in 1952. Although there have been more recent, unconfirmed reports, an aerial survey in 1973 found fishing activity throughout the region and no signs of seals. Subsequent searches have failed to locate it.

1950s
Lesser Bilby
(Macrotis leucura)

Last Record: 1950s. Distribution: Central Australia.

The lesser bilby, which was the size of a young rabbit, was an inhabitant of Australia's driest deserts. It was recorded as a living animal on just a handful of occasions between its discovery in 1887 and its extinction in the 1950s. Numbers of the bilby seem to have been moderately high on Cooncherie Station in the summer of 1932, where Hedley Herbert Finlayson collected a dozen specimens. These were all caught by an Aboriginal helper who 'seldom returned without 2 or 3 after a morning's work and I suspect many found their way to the cooking fires as well'. These were, however, the last to be collected alive.

Unlike most members of the bandicoot group to which it belongs, the lesser bilby was a carnivore, and native rodents were recorded among its prey. And unlike the gentle and still surviving common bilby, it had a nasty temperament. Finlayson noted it was 'fierce and intractable, and repulsed the most tactful attempts to handle them by repeated savage snapping bites and harsh hissing sounds'. It burrowed only in sand dunes, constructing burrows two or three metres deep, closing the entrance with loose sand by day. It was strictly nocturnal, twins were standard, and reproduction may have been non-seasonal.

The last recorded specimen consists of a skull picked up below a wedgetailed eagle's nest by P. Hanisch at Steele Gap in the Simpson Desert, Northern Territory, in 1967. The bone was still quite new, and was estimated to be less than fifteen years old.

1953
Ilin Island Cloudrunner
(*Crateromys paulus*)

Last Record: 4 April 1953. Distribution: Ilin Island, Philippines.

The cloudrunners are fluffy-coated rats, kitten- to cat-sized, with bushy tails and are found only on certain of the Philippine islands. There are four species, most of which inhabit the high mountain forests. The living species emerge from tree hollows at night to feed on a variety of fruits and leaves.

The Ilin Island cloudrunner is known from a single specimen, collected by Pablo Soriano and presented to the National Museum of Natural History in Washington D.C. by Eduardo Gelena. No locality or habitat information was recorded when the specimen was captured. Ilin is a small island located off the southern tip of Mindoro in the Philippines. It was visited by biologists in 1988, who found that the island's forests (presumably the species' habitat) had been destroyed by human activity. They could locate no evidence of the rat's survival.

Little Swan Island Hutia

(*Geocapromys thoracatus*)

Last Record: 1955. Distribution: Little Swan Island off North-eastern Honduras, Caribbean.

There are five species of hutias of the genus *Geocapromys*, only two of which survive to the present, and two of which are known only from skeletal remains. Rodents of the Caribbean region, they are distantly related to porcupines, and are between one and two kilograms in weight. They are slow-moving and guinea-pig like, emerging from caves and limestone crevices to forage on bark, small twigs and leaves.

It seems possible that the ancestors of the Little Swan Island hutias were carried to the island from Jamaica between 5000 and 7000 years ago. If so, it should probably be recognised as a subspecies of the Jamaican hutia (*G. browni*). It seemed to be relatively common in the early twentieth century, but disappeared following a severe hurricane in 1955. House cats were introduced to the island shortly thereafter, sealing the fate of any survivors.

Crescent Nailtail Wallaby

(Onychogalea lunata)

Last Record: 1956. Distribution: Western and Central Australia.

The woodlands and scrubs of the west and centre of Australia were once home to the silky-furred crescent nailtail wallaby. The genus to which it belongs is distinguished, as its common name suggests, by the presence of a horny spur at the tip of the tail. The function of this appendage is still unknown.

The crescent nailtail was the smallest member of the genus, resembling a hare in size. One of its more peculiar characteristics was its propensity to seek refuge in a hollow tree when chased, entering at the bottom, and clambering up until it appeared at an opening high above.

The very last specimen ever collected as a living animal was caught in a dingo trap on the Nullarbor Plain in 1927 or 1928. The 'dogger' who caught the animal, a Mr W. A. Wills, sent it to Taronga Zoo in Sydney, from where it made its way to the Australian Museum. Wills was still alive in June 1984 when the Western Australian Department of Land Management decided to conduct a survey of the Nullarbor Plain. They arranged to speak with him, in the hope he would recall something of the creatures' habits and distribution. Wills, unfortunately, became so nervous at the prospect of the interview that the night before it was to take place he escaped from his retirement home, and drove his car through the night to visit his brother in Queensland!

The crescent nailtail wallaby remained common, even in agricultural districts in the south-west of Western Australia, until around 1900. By 1908, however, it had begun a steep decline and the last record from the region dates to that year. It survived in the more arid parts of its distribution until the 1950s. Just what caused its disappearance is still debated, but the spread of the fox seems to be correlated with its loss and may have been the principal factor.

1962

Bavarian Pine-vole

(Microtis bavaricus)

Last Record: 1962. Distribution: Italian and Bavarian Alps, Europe.

The voles are among the most successful of all mammals. There are sixty-five species, distributed throughout Europe, northern and central Asia and North America. The Bavarian pine-vole, here shown at actual size, was found at elevations of between 600 and 1000 metres in the districts of Garmisch-Partenkirschen in the Bavarian Alps and in the Tyrol, Italy. It differed from the common pine-vole in its chromosomes and aspects of its skull and teeth.

The moist meadow that formed its only known habitat was destroyed by construction of a hospital during the 1980s. No specimen has been collected since 1962, and just twenty-three specimens reside in museums around the world.

1965
Greater Short-tailed Bat
(Mystacina robusta)

*Last Record: April 1965. Distribution: Prehistorically, North and South Islands, New Zealand;
Historically, Small Islands off Stewart Island, New Zealand.*

New Zealand was home to only three land mammals before the arrival of the Maori, and all were bats. Two species belonged to a unique New Zealand bat family, of which the greater short-tailed bat (following page) was the larger. The short-tailed bats are most peculiar creatures. They are the only bats that are as adept at scrambling along the ground as they are at flying, and have pouches on the sides of their bodies for their wings to fold into. With their wings hidden away they can race through burrows or scrub with the alacrity of shrews or mice.

Fossils indicate that before the arrival of the Maori the greater short-tailed bat was widespread throughout New Zealand. In historic times, however, it was known only from one dubious record from the South Island, and from several small islands off Stewart Island in the far south. There, the bats used the burrows of seabirds as roosts. They flew slowly, never rising more than two or three metres off the ground. They took nectar from flowering plants, and were probably also partly carnivorous, taking fat and meat off muttonbirds left out to dry overnight, as well as eating nestling birds.

The very last refuges of these unique bats were on Solomon and Big South Cape islands, which remained rat-free until a remarkably late date. The bats thrived until 1962 or 1963, when black rats arrived aboard fishing vessels. Almost immediately the unique fauna of the islands began to vanish, and the greater short-tailed bat was among the victims. The last one seen was caught in a mist net on Solomon Island in April 1965.

1972

Slender Bush Wren

(Xenicus longipes)

Last Record: 1972. Distribution: North, South, Stewart and Nearby Islands, New Zealand.

The slender bush wren was a small, poorly flighted wren-like bird belonging to a family that is entirely restricted to New Zealand. Curiously, although it is considered to belong to a group that comprises the most ancient of songbirds, it was largely silent, having no song, just giving faint rasping sounds as it foraged, using its long, slender bill for gleaning insects. It built its nests in cavities among tree roots, in fallen logs or clumps of ferns. Both parents incubated the eggs. In its habits and ecology it was more like a mouse than a bird, and in New Zealand, which lacked mammals except for a few bats, these wrens may have evolved to fill the ecological niche occupied by small rodents elsewhere.

It was rare on the North Island at the time of European contact, the last specimens being collected there around 1850. It persisted on the South Island until around 1968. Its last stronghold, however, was Big South Cape Island off Stewart Island, but when rats reached the island in 1962 it went into a rapid decline. Before it disappeared in 1967 wildlife rangers had rescued six birds, which they transferred to nearby, rat-free Kaimohu Island. Two were seen there in 1972, but since 1977 they have been seen no more. Its extinction went almost entirely unremarked by the New Zealand public, who remained as silent as the bird itself about the tragedy that had befallen the nation.

1973

Barred-winged Rail

(Nesoclopeus poecilopterus)

Last Record: 5.35 p.m., 28 June 1973. Distribution: Viti Levu and Ovalau, Fiji.

The barred-winged rail was a secretive, poorly flighted and evidently nocturnal bird around the size of a half-grown chicken. It inhabited dense swamps and taro gardens. Neither its voice nor food were recorded, though some eggs were collected last century, which are cream-brown in colour, with purplish and red blotches. It is known from less than a dozen museum specimens, all collected during the nineteenth century.

The species was long considered to be extinct until D. T. Holyoak visited Fiji in 1973 and carried out intensive bird surveys for two months. He sighted a barred-winged rail in the Vundiawa area of Viti Levu. It was seen in a 'small valley with old overgrown taro and banana plantations among thickets of bamboo and tall ferns under the cover of tall, well-spaced trees'. Despite much searching, he found no evidence of the species on Taveuni. The species appears to have been rare even before European contact, but the introductions of the mongoose and brown and black rats to Fiji are doubtless responsible for its further decline.

1974

Guam Flying-fox

(Pteropus tokudae)

Last Record: June 1974. Distribution: Guam, Marianas Islands, Micronesia.

Guam is the largest and southernmost of the Marianas Islands, and once was home to a diverse and unique fauna, including the tiny Guam flying-fox (following page). Evidently it was always rare. It was first recorded in 1931, its obscurity before that time perhaps relating to the fact that it roosted with the larger and much more common Marianas flying-fox.

The last specimen collected was a female found roosting at Tarague cliff in March 1967. She was accompanied by a young one that escaped capture. Although a probable sighting was made in June 1974, a survey during 1987 failed to reveal the presence of the species, and local hunters questioned in the 1970s presumed it to be very rare or extinct. Nothing is known of its biology. Hunting or habitat change may have been factors in its extinction.

Since the loss of this flying-fox, Guam has experienced a cascade of extinctions brought about by the introduction of the brown tree snake (*Boiga irregularis*). As a result its forests are now largely silent, the island having lost many of its pollinators and fruit dispersers. The fate of Guam's ecology in the wake of such destruction should be of much interest to biologists, as many regions may come to resemble it in future.

Philippine Bare-backed Fruit-bat

(Dobsonia chapmani)

Last Record: Early 1980s. Distribution: Negros Island, Philippines.

The bare-backed fruit-bats possess wings that meet along the midline of their bodies, making them exceptionally agile fliers. The group has its distribution centred on the island of New Guinea, but one species, the Philippine bare-backed fruit-bat (previous page), was until recently found north-west, on the island of Negros in the Philippines.

Bare-backed fruit-bats roost in caves, in areas where a little light still penetrates the gloom. The Philippine species was once so great in number that it left piles of guano large enough to be used by farmers as fertiliser. Although it was hunted at its roost by the guano miners, it was relatively safe until its forest home began to disappear.

Just fifty years ago around 60 per cent of Negros Island was covered in forest. A government eager to promote development introduced a subsidy for sugar producers, and by the mid-1980s all of the lowland forest was gone, replaced by sugar-cane plantations. Today the unique Philippines bare-backed fruit-bat and its piles of guano have vanished, both sacrificed to sugar-cane production. Given the massive rate of population increase and habitat destruction that the Philippines is currently experiencing, it will surely not be the last mammal of this region to become extinct.

1989
Atitlán Grebe
(Podilymbus gigas)

Last Record: 1989. Distribution: Lake Atitlán, Guatemala.

There is a convention in biology that one must wait fifty years after a last sighting before a species is proclaimed extinct. Some species, however, have such restricted distributions, or are so well known, that their extinction is evident soon after a last sighting is made. Such was the case with the Atitlán grebe (following page), a giant, nearly flightless water bird that inhabited a single place, the 360-metre-deep Lake Atitlán in the Guatemalan highlands. Known to the local inhabitants as *mama poc*, the grebe had presumably cruised the lake's waters since the species had evolved before the last ice age.

Until about 1965 it enjoyed a relatively stable population of around 800. Soon thereafter, however, a series of changes occurred which disadvantaged the birds. Both small- and large-mouth bass were introduced into the lake in 1958, and these voracious predators greatly reduced the crab and fish populations upon which the grebe depended. By 1975 the grebe population had fallen to around 210 individuals, and a conservation program was instituted to protect the species by legislation, community education and habitat preservation. The campaign was inadequate, however, for along with the bass other changes were afoot that would destroy the species. The water level was falling, and would drop over six metres in the thirty-five years after 1965. Reed-cutters were destroying valuable habitat and the lake was invaded by the related and widespread common pied-billed grebe.

Researchers surveyed the grebe population by playing a recording of the call of the male at night during the breeding season. Any male hearing the call of another male would respond, giving an accurate estimate of the number of breeding pairs. The trouble was, the calls of the pied-billed and giant grebes were very similar, and the researchers did not realise that a second species had invaded the lake. By the late 1970s they were predicting a resurgence in numbers of the giant grebe, until one day they approached some— and, to their horror, they saw the birds fly away. They then realised that they had been counting not the flightless giant grebe, but its smaller, flighted pied-billed relative.

The pied-billed grebe found the degraded lake much to its liking, and by the mid-1980s was breeding year-round and producing multiple broods. It may have hybridised with the giant grebe, thus reducing its breeding success, or may have simply outcompeted it. By 1989 just two pairs of giant grebe inhabited the lake, and none have been seen since.

Appendix

A list of species the reader might reasonably expect to find illustrated
in this book, and the reason for their exclusion.

Taxonomic uncertainty

Desert Bandicoot *(Perameles eremiana)*
Percy Islands Flying-fox *(Pteropus brunneus)*
Okinawa Flying-fox *(Pteropus loochoensis)*
Panay Giant Fruit-bat *(Acerodon lucifer)*
Barbados Raccoon *(Procyon gloveralleni)*
Quagga *(Equus quagga quagga)*
Schomburgk's Deer *(Cervus schomburgki)*
Arabian Gazelle *(Gazella arabica)*

New Zealand Little Bittern *(Ixobrychus novaezelandiae)*
New Zealand Quail *(Coturnix novaezelandiae)*
Dieffenbach's Rail *(Gallirallus dieffenbachii)*
Cooper's Sandpiper *(Pisobia cooperi)*
Lord Howe Gerygone *(Gerygone insularis)*
Tasman Starling *(Aplonis fusca)*

Appearance insufficiently known

Central Hare-wallaby *(Lagorchestes asomatus)*
Long-eared Bat *(Nyctophilus howensis)*
Atalaye Nesophontes *(Nesophontes hypomicrus)*
Western Cuban Nesophontes *(Nesophontes micrus)*
Saint Michel Nesophontes *(Nesophontes paramicrus)*
Haitian Nesophontes *(Nesophontes zamicrus)*
Solenodon *(Solenodon marcanoi)*
Sardinian Pika *(Prolagus sardus)*
rodent *(Geocapromys columbianus)*
rodent *(Hexolobodon phenax)*
rodent *(Isolobodon montanus)*
rodent *(Plagiodontia araeum)*
rodent *(Plagiodontia ipnaeum)*
rodent *(Plagiodontia velozi)*
rodent *(Rhizoplagiodontia lemkei)*
rodent *(Boromys offella)*
rodent *(Boromys torrei)*
rodent *(Brotomys contractus)*

rodent *(Brotomys voratus)*
rodent *(Heteropsomys antillensis)*
rodent *(Heteropsomys insulans)*
rodent *(Puertoricomys corozalus)*
rodent *(Sphiggurus pallidus)*
rodent *(Amblyrhiza inundata)*
rodent *(Clidomys osborni)*
rodent *(Clidomys parvus)*
rodent *(Elasmodontomys obliquus)*
rodent *(Quemisia gravis)*
rodent *(Canariomys tamarani)*
rodent *(Coryphomys buhleri)*
Florida Rat *(Solomys salamonis)*
Darling Downs Hopping-mouse *(Notomys mordax)*
Great Hopping-mouse *(Notomys* sp.*)*
Basalt Plains Mouse *(Pseudomys* sp.*)*
King Island Emu *(Dromaius ater)*
Kangaroo Island Emu *(Dromaius baudinianus)*
Réunion Flightless Ibis *(Borbonibis latipes)*

Mauritius Night-heron (*Nycticorax mauritianus*)

Rodrigues Night-heron (*Nycticorax megacephalus*)

Mauritian Shelduck (*Alopochen mauritianus*)

Amsterdam Island wigeon (*Anas marecula*)

Mauritian Duck (*Anas theodori*)

Chatham Islands Swan (*Cygnus sumnerensis*)

Mauritian Red Rail (*Aphanapteryx bonasia*)

Rodrigues Rail (*Aphanapteryx leguati*)

Ascension Flightless Crake (*Atlantisia elpenor*)

Tahiti Rail (*Gallirallus pacificus*)

Mascarene Coot (*Fulica newtoni*)

Rodrigues Solitaire (*Pezophaps solitaria*)

Réunion Solitaire (*Raphus solitarius*)

Rodrigues Pigeon (*Alectroenas rodericana*)

Mauritius Grey Parrot (*Lophopsittacus bensoni*)

Mauritius Parrot (*Lophopsittacus mauritianus*)

Rodrigues Parrot (*Necropsittacus rodericanus*)

Rodrigues Little Owl (*Athene murivora*)

Mauritian Owl (*Scops commersoni*)

Rodrigues Starling (*Necrospar rodericanus*)

gecko (*Phelsuma edwardnewtonii*)

As *A Gap in Nature* was going to press we discovered that three spirit-preserved specimens are held in collections of the Natural History Museum, London.

gecko (*Phelsuma gigas*)

skink (*Leiolopisma mauritiana*)

skink (*Gongylomorphus borbonicus*)

turtle (*Cylindraspis indica*)

turtle (*Cylindraspis inepta*)

turtle (*Cylindraspis peltastes*)

turtle (*Cylindraspis triserrata*)

turtle (*Cylindraspis vosmaeri*)

As *A Gap in Nature* was going to press we discovered that a stuffed specimen is held in a collection of the Museé National d'Histoire Naturelle, Paris.

Extinction not certain

San Salvador Rice-rat (*Nesoromys swarthi*)

Emperor Rat (*Uromys imperator*)

Little Pig-rat (*Uromys porculus*)

Puerto Rican Flower-bat (*Phyllonycteris major*)

Miller's Myotis (*Myotis milleri*)

Flat-headed Myotis (*Myotis planiceps*)

New Guinea Long-eared Bat (*Pharotis imogene*)

Colombian Grebe (*Podiceps andinus*)

Javanese Lapwing (*Vanellus macropterus*)

Akialoa (*Hemignathus obscurus*)

Molokai Creeper (*Paroreomyza flammea*)

Saint Croix Racer (*Alsophis sancticrucis*)

colubrid snake (*Alsophis ater*)

colubrid snake (*Alsophis sanctaecrucis*)

colubrid snake (*Dromicus cursor*)

colubrid snake (*Dromicus ornatus*)

boiid snake (*Bolyeria multicarinata*)

Eastwood's Long-tailed Seps (*Tetradactylus eastwoodae*)

Jamaica Giant Galliwasp (*Celestus occiduus*)

Martinique Giant Ameiva (*Ameiva major*)

teiid lizard (*Ameiva cineracea*)

iguanid lizard (*Cyclura collei*)

iguanid lizard (*Leiocephalus eremitus*)

iguanid lizard (*Leiocephalus herminieri*)

turtles (*Geochelone* spp.)

Bibliography

Andersen, K., *Catalogue of the Chiroptera in the Collection of the British Museum vol. 1: Megachiroptera*, British Museum of Natural History, London, 1912.

Bauer, A. M. & Russell, A. P., '*Hoplodactylus delcourti* n. sp. (Reptilia: Gekkonidae), the Largest Known Gecko', *New Zealand Journal of Zoology* vol. 13, 1986, pp. 141–48.

Bauer, A. M. & Sadlier, R. A., *The Herpetofauna of New Caledonia*, Society for the Study of Amphibians and Reptiles, Ithaca, New York, 2000.

Burbidge, A. A., 'Crescent Nailtail Wallaby' in *The Mammals of Australia*, R. Strahan ed., Reed Books, Chatswood, 1995, pp. 359–60.

Burt, W. H., 'Descriptions of Heretofore Unknown Mammals from Islands in the Gulf of California, Mexico', *Transactions of the San Diego Society of Natural History* vol. 7, 1932, pp. 161–82.

Cade, T. T. & Temple, S. A., 'Management of Threatened Bird Species: Evaluation of the Hands-on Approach', *Ibis* vol. 137, 1995, pp. 161–72.

Corbet, G. & Ovenden, D., *The Mammals of Britain and Europe*, Collins, London, 1980.

Dann, J. C. ed., *The Nagle Journal: A Diary of the Life of Jacob Nagle, Sailor, from the Year 1775 to 1841*, Weidenfeld & Nicolson, New York, 1988.

Dixon, J., 'Big-eared Hopping-mouse' in *The Mammals of Australia*, R. Strahan ed., Reed Books, Chatswood, 1995, pp. 578–79.

Dixon, J., 'Gould's Mouse' in *The Mammals of Australia*, R. Strahan ed., Reed Books, Chatswood, 1995, pp. 600–1.

Ehrlich, P. R., Dobkin, D. S. & Wheye, D., *Birds in Jeopardy: The Imperiled and Extinct Birds of the United States and Canada*, Stanford University Press, California, 1992.

Finlayson, H. H., *The Red Centre: Man and Beast in the Heart of Australia*, Angus & Robertson, Sydney, 1935.

Flannery, T. F., *Australia's Vanishing Mammals*, Reader's Digest Press, Sydney, 1990.

Flannery, T. F., *Mammals of the South West Pacific and Moluccan Islands*, Reed Books, Chatswood, 1995.

Fuller, E., *Extinct Birds*, Viking/Rainbird, London, 1987.

Gill, B. & Martinson, P., *New Zealand's Extinct Birds*, Random Century, Auckland, 1991.

Graves, G. R., 'Relic of a Lost World: A New Species of Sunangel (Trochilidae: *Heliangelus*) from Bogota', *Auk* vol. 110, 1993, pp. 1–8.

Graves, G. R. & Olsen S. L., '*Chlorostilbon bracei* Lawrence: An Extinct Species of Hummingbird from New Providence, Bahamas', *Auk* vol. 104, 1987, pp. 296–302.

Greenaway, J. C., *Extinct and Vanishing Birds of the World*, Dover, New York, 1967.

Greer, A. E., 'On the Evolution of the Giant Cape Verde Scincid Lizard *Macroscincus coctei*', *Journal of Natural History* vol. 10, 1976, pp. 691–712.

Guiler, E., *Thylacine: The Tragedy of the Tasmanian Tiger*, Melbourne University Press, Melbourne, 1985.

Harper, F., *Extinct and Vanishing Mammals of the Old World*, American Committee for International Wildlife Protection special publication no. 12, New York, 1945.

Heaney, L. R. & Regalado, J. C., *Vanishing Treasures of the Philippine Rain Forest*, Field Museum, Chicago, 1998.

Holyoak, D. T., 'Notes on the Birds of Viti Levu and Taveuni, Fiji', *Emu* vol. 79, 1979, pp. 7–18.

Hunter, L. A., 'Status of the Endemic Atitlán Grebe of Guatemala: Is It Extinct?', *Condor* vol. 90, 1988, pp. 906–12.

Hutton, I., *Birds of Lord Howe Island*, self-published, Melbourne, 1990.

Johnson, K. A., 'Thylacomyidae', chapter 25 in *The Fauna of Australia* vol. 1a, Australian Government Publishing Service, Canberra, 1987.

Johnson, K. A. & Burbidge, A. A., 'Pig-footed Bandicoot' in *The Mammals of Australia*, R. Strahan ed., Reed Books, Chatswood, 1995, pp. 170–71.

Johnson, K. A. & Southgate, R. I., 'Presence and Former Status of Bandicoots in the Northern Territory' in *Bandicoots & Bilbies*, J. H. Seebeck, P. R. Brown, R. L. Wallis & C. M. Kemper eds, Surrey Beatty & Sons, New South Wales, 1990, pp. 85–92.

Kitchener, D., 'Broad-faced Potoroo' in *The Mammals of Australia*, R. Strahan ed., Reed Books, Chatswood, 1995, pp. 300–1.

Kowalski, K. & Rzebik-Kowalska, B., *Mammals of Algeria*, Ossolineum, Krakow, 1991.

Krefft, G., 'On the Vertebrated Animals of the Lower Murray and Darling, Their Habits, Economy, and Geographical Distribution', *Transactions of the Philosophical Society of New South Wales*, 1862, pp. 1–33.

Lidicker, W. Z. ed., *Rodents: A World Survey of Species of Conservation Concern*, IUCN, Switzerland, 1985.

Musser, G. G. & Gordon, L. K., 'A New Species of *Crateromys* (Muridae) from the Philippines', *Journal of Mammalogy* vol. 62, 1981, pp. 513–25.

Oliver, P. ed., *The Voyages Made by the* Sieur *D. B. to the Islands Dauphine or Madagascar & Bourbon or Mascarenne in the Years 1669, 70, 71 & 72*, David Nutt, London, 1893.

Osgood, W. H., 'A New Rodent from the Galapagos Islands', *Field Museum of Natural History* vol. 17, Chicago, 1929, p. 23.

Paddle, R. N., *The Last Tasmanian Tiger: The History and Extinction of the Thylacine*, Cambridge University Press, Melbourne, 2000.

Purcell, R., *Swift As a Shadow: Extinct and Endangered Animals*, Mariner Books, Boston, 1999.

Robinson, A. C., 'Lesser Stick-nest Rat' in *The Mammals of Australia*, R. Strahan ed., Reed Books, Chatswood, 1995, pp. 558–59.

Robinson, A. C. & Young, M. C., *The Toolache Wallaby (*Macropus greyi *Waterhouse)*, Department of Environment & Planning special publication no. 2, 1983.

Rosen, H. ed., *An Account in Two Volumes of Two Voyages to the South Seas by Captain Jules S.-C. d'Urville*, Melbourne University Press, Melbourne, 1987.

Rounsevell, D. E. & Mooney, N., 'Thylacine' in *The Mammals of Australia*, R. Strahan ed., Reed Books, Chatswood, 1995, pp. 164–65.

Sadlier, R. A., 'A Review of the Scincid Lizards of New Caledonia', *Records of the Australian Museum* vol. 39, 1986, pp. 1–66.

Smithers, R. H. N., *The Mammals of the Southern African Subregion*, University of Pretoria, South Africa, 1983.

Steller, Georg Wilhelm, *Journal of a Voyage with Bering, 1741–1742*, O. W. Frost ed., Stanford University Press, California, 1988.

Strahan, R., 'Eastern Hare-wallaby' in *The Mammals of Australia*, R. Strahan ed., Reed Books, Chatswood, 1995, pp. 319–20.

Watling, D., *Birds of Fiji, Tonga and Samoa*, Millwood Press, Wellington, 1982.

Watts, C. H. S. & Aslin, H. J., *The Rodents of Australia*, Angus & Robertson, Sydney, 1981.

Index